HOW TO WRITE A FANTASY NOVEL

Unlock Your Imagination With This Step-By-Step Guide To Crafting Compelling Plots And Memorable Characters

HACKNEY AND JONES

Copyright © 2023 by Hackney and Jones

All rights reserved.

No part of this book may be reproduced in any form or by any electronic or mechanical means, including information storage and retrieval systems, without written permission from the author, except for the use of brief quotations in a book review.

Contents

This Workbook Goes With The Guidebook You Are Reading	vii
Preface By Vicky Jones	ix
Introduction	xv
What Is The Secret?	xvii

Part I
The Genre Bundle

The Genre Bundle – Fantasy Fiction	3
The Words Most Frequently Used In Bestselling Book Descriptions	6
Character Names And Roles	9
Events	12
Locations	14
TITLES AND SUBTITLES	17
S.E.O – Search Engine Optimisation	20
Do's And Don't's Of The Genre	24
FANTASY TROPES AND STEREOTYPES	28
What is a trope?	28
What is a stereotype?	30
Power Words	33
More Plot Twists To Add To Your Ending	39
Characters Part 2 - Develop Them Further	44
INTERNAL AND EXTERNAL GOALS	46
Internal goals	46
External goals	48
The Final Amazing Novel Summary	51

Part II
The Complete Plan: Your Novel Outline

WHY THREE ACTS AND TEN CHAPTERS?	57
The Three-Act Structure	57
ACT 1	59
Chapter 1	60
Chapter 2	65
Chapter 3	67
ACT 2	70
Chapter 4	71
Chapter 5	73
Chapter 6	76
ACT 3	78
Chapter 7	78
Chapter 8	80
Chapter 9	81
Chapter 10	82
Word Count	85

Part III
After You Have Written Your Novel

HOW TO WRITE A SYNOPSIS	89
So, how do you write a strong synopsis?	91
HOW TO WRITE A BLURB	94
So, how do you write a strong blurb?	95
PLOTTING – USEFUL TOOLS TO HELP YOU FURTHER	99
Scrivener	99
Plottr	101
Bestselling Book Covers	103
SELF-PUBLISHING VS TRADITIONAL PUBLISHING	113
Self-publishing	113
Traditional publishing	117
Self-publishing Vs Traditional publishing – the pros and cons of each	118

Bonuses	121
Course Offer	125
Contact Us	131
This Workbook Goes With The Guidebook You Are Reading	133

This Workbook Goes With The Guidebook You Are Reading

The ultimate novel writing planner with a secret formula to hook your readers in from the very first page. Effortlessly create a magical story from scratch using creative writing templates that will catapult you from blank page to publishing a fantasy novel that sells.

Preface
By Vicky Jones

Do you have a bucket list?

I do.

When I turned 30, I made a bucket list of hundreds of things I wanted to achieve. And to be fair, I ticked off quite a few of them in the following 10 years alone, including:

- Alaska
- Mongolia
- Iceland
- Hawaii
- L.A.
- Croatia
- Cambodia
- Vietnam

It has been life-changing and I recommend you start a bucket list. It doesn't have to include travel. Some of mine were academic, like getting my degree in Criminology and Psychology.

Writing a novel was on my bucket list.

I'm a creative person, and a songwriter, so I thought that writing a novel was an extended version of writing a song.

Songs are mini-stories, right?

To an extent, writing songs has helped me with writing a novel, as each word in a song has to move the story forward. There's no room for fluff in a song.

But…

I didn't know the actual practicality of turning an idea into a full-blown novel.

So, I came up with some ideas, started writing, had a rough idea of an ending and saw how I got on.

I didn't get far.

I started putting off writing because I couldn't see a way forward through writer's block.

Where would each scene fit? I couldn't see through the fog.

I remember consoling myself *'writing a novel won't get ticked off the bucket list, but that's ok…'*

It wasn't ok. I wanted to have my book out there in the world and for people to be able to read it.

Then, a lovely lady called Sharon started a writing group which Claire and I joined. Sharon helped us get inspired by creating writing competitions each month.

I found I was confident with writing *short* stories, but I had a block when it came to writing a full-length novel.

Why?

Because I was writing from MY perspective.

I needed a way to make sure my novel flowed and was exciting to the readers also.

At first, I was content to write one novel, but that was proving to be my Everest.

I came across a video on YouTube that changed my life. It was by the Oscar-winning screenwriter Dustin Lance Black. He wrote the screenplay for the film 'Milk.' In this video, he shares his screenwriting process.

He uses index/note cards. Each index card represents one singular scene.

This blew my mind.

Rather than 'write a novel', he wrote index cards full of exciting, meaningful scenes. It broke his screenplay down into manageable pieces so it was less overwhelming to write.

I thought, *'what if I tried this with novel writing?'*

Using this method, you can 'see' your novel appear in front of you. You can add a filler scene wherever needed so that the novel moves into the next scene.

I got excited.

I went to my writing group as usual. One month, the writing prompt was 'vending machine'.

What?

The idea was to stretch your imagination and bring you out of your comfort zone.

I came up with an idea where two people 'met' at the vending machine in secret, and if they got caught it would be dangerous. I wrote an idea for the writing competition, but then I came up with another idea for my bucket list novel.

That idea then developed into two people meeting up in secret in the 1950s American Deep South.

Thus the idea for our debut novel **'Meet Me At 10'** was born. Out of all the books we've written, this is my favourite.

I would now use Dustin Lance Black's process to write it.

I came up with my own prompts so that the novel included all the things a book (and a movie) would need. These elements included:

- Character arcs
- Inciting events
- Plot twists

I loved every second of moving the index cards around to create my story. I made sure to take the readers on a ride, rather than before where I was writing to get to the end. I put the readers first.

I now had a workable process for novel writing.

What was the result?

Our debut novel **'Meet Me At 10'** became a bestseller in its category, and the reviews speak for themselves.

For each following novel, we streamlined the process, improved it even more, and taught others how we do it.

This is what this guide to the workbook is about.

You are getting that process explained to you.

We hope you have the same amount of enjoyment and success as we did.

- *Vicky Jones*

Introduction

Thank you for buying **'How To Write A Fantasy Novel'**. We have designed this guide to go hand-in-hand with the Fantasy Fiction Workbook below:

This guide will help you to understand the templates in the above workbook. It will help you to discover the secrets to writing a creative and magical fantasy novel. We'll take you step-by-step through the process of filling in the templates in the workbook. The goal is to help you to create books that sell fast.

We are Vicky and Claire from **'Hackney and Jones Publishing'**. This series of workbooks draw upon our experiences in the self-publishing industry. We have gained this knowledge from our years producing fiction and non-fiction books.

We have made so many mistakes along the way that we wanted to stop you from making the same ones. So, we devised this series of no-fuss, zero-fluff workbooks.

Due to feedback from our readers, we have decided to create workbooks for other genres also. These are:

- Romance
- Sci-fi
- Historical Fiction
- Young Adult
- Military
- Women's Fiction
- Fantasy
- Paranormal
- Horror
- Cozy Mystery
- Psychological
- Suspense/Thriller
- Action and Adventure
- Erotica

So, what is the secret to writing winning fiction? Let us talk you through that.

What Is The Secret?

If you want to write a book that sells, you must give your readers the rollercoaster. What do we mean by this?

To understand this image, we must picture our readers queuing up for a rollercoaster ride. As they look up at the track they understand there will be bumps, drops and speed corners along the way. But they will still scream with surprise when they are riding the rollercoaster!

Why is this?

Because they WANT to FEEL the drops and EXPERIENCE the speed corners. That's what they have paid for.

You must think of your book as the same.

Give your readers this same experience and they will rip your next book off the shelf. Make them addicted to your bumps, drops and speed corners in your fantasy novel and you will have a fan for life.

Our biggest piece of advice for you, before you plan your next best-seller, is to put your reader first. From concept to completion, the most important person for the success of your book is the reader. Consider your target audience. If you write fantasy fiction because you enjoy reading it yourself, think about what YOU would want.

When we read non-fiction books, it's sometimes to learn a skill. I don't want to hear all about the author unless it's an autobiography. If it's a fiction book I'm reading I want it to entertain me. I want the escapism that a well-plotted, well-written book promises me.

When we buy a fiction book we hope for exciting plot twists. We cross our fingers for a great, satisfying ending. We pray to the fiction gods that it will be one we don't guess until the very end. We expect villains, 'damsels in distress,' and also a full array of helpers and confidantes.

We expect all this, as readers, before we even open the book cover. And when you get what you hoped for you feel relieved as a reader. In safe hands, even, with this author.

You.

Your readers want to sit down, strap themselves in and get ready to experience the ride of their lives. And it's your responsibility as their new favourite author to take them on that ride. They are investing their time in your novel. They want the rollercoaster they have paid for. Give them the ride of their lives.

How? By following the steps we will cover in this guide to writing winning fantasy fiction.

What you will need to plan your fantasy novel is our workbook.

If you follow our winning formula, you will give your readers what they want. Once you complete the templates in the workbook you will have a clear novel outline. This will be easy for you to start writing from. As a result, your novel will:

- Be well-plotted
- Be well-researched
- Have plot twists in all the right places
- Have an exciting ending

This cannot fail to put you amongst the bestsellers in your genre. Your readers will be so overjoyed by the brilliantness of your novel. They will rave about it to their friends, colleagues and family. You will also receive amazing reviews, leading more readers to discover you.

What author would say no to that? Not you, eh? That's why you're here, right?

This is extremely important. By understanding what readers want, we can discover what they are spending their money on.

We've looked in detail at what people are actually searching for online. We were curious to know what types of fantasy fiction sub-niche themes are making the most money.

Using a piece of software called 'Publisher Rocket', we found the most common sub-niches in crime were:

- Fantasy novel for adults
- Fantasy young adult
- Fantasy novel for kids 9-12
- Fantasy book for teens
- Fantasy adventure book
- Fantasy romance book

Make sure that, if it's relevant to your story idea, you include some of these words in your **subtitles**. You want your book to get found by your readers in online searches.

How can this procedure help you? Well, you might know you want to write a fantasy novel, but now you know that 'fantasy books for teens' is a big seller. You might now want to aim your novel at that target audience. For the purposes of the workbook, we chose *'fantasy adventure novel for young adults.'*

You know that sub-niche is getting searched for so you know that people are spending money on it. Before you've even written a single word of your novel, you're already onto a winner.

For your next step in planning your idea, you should pick which area you want to focus on out of the above themes.

The beauty of our planning system is there are so many different combinations to choose from.

Remember, you can write more than one book for each suggestion. The possibilities are endless!

So, let's get straight into the first chapter of the workbook.

PART I

The Genre Bundle

The Genre Bundle - Fantasy Fiction

The Genre Bundle is our secret weapon in the fight against the dreaded writer's block. Whether you are a die-hard plotter or a free-as-a-bird pantser, this has something for both. It will help you to plan a solid summary of your novel and give you the creative freedom to add elements as you see fit.

In this section, we will cover all the elements you will need to consider to plan a solid summary of your novel. We have compiled The Genre Bundle by looking at the top 50 books in the fantasy genre. Throughout this guide, we've used Amazon's top 50 best-selling fantasy books as the basis of our research.

We have taken a deep dive into the elements that make them best-selling.

This includes:

- The Words Most Frequently Used In Bestselling Book Descriptions
- Character Names And Roles
- Events

- Locations
- Titles And Subtitles
- Do's And Don't's Of The Genre
- Fantasy Tropes And Stereotypes
- Power Words
- More Plot Twists To Add To Your Ending
- Characters Part 2 - Develop Them Further
- Internal And External Goals

At the end of this section, you will put all your thoughts together into one amazing novel summary.

Before we expand on the sections above, we need to establish a definition of what fantasy fiction is.

Fantasy fiction is a genre of storytelling that typically involves elements of magic, mythical creatures, and supernatural events. It often takes place in a fantastical world or alternate universe, and the stories often focus on heroes who embark on quests and adventures.

Fantasy stories can be set in a variety of different worlds and can be told in many different formats, including novels, movies, television shows, and video games. In general, fantasy fiction is known for its imagination and creativity, as it allows writers to explore new and exciting ideas that might not be possible in the real world.

Let's talk for a moment about writing-to-market. Some die-hard "pantsers" claim writing-to-market takes all the creativity out of writing.

This is not true.

Writing-to-market is nothing to do with the actual quality of the book. It involves looking at what type of book is selling and the themes it involves. Then you write a book in this vein, but with your own take on it. This way you are giving your readers what they want.

Trends come and go, and hopping on one is not always a bad thing. Quality lives forever, which is what your book will be.

Especially if your goal or intention is to make money from your writing. We see it as a trade - readers get a book they know they will enjoy as it is in the niche they can't get enough of at the moment. Authors get a sale. Simple. Readers want entertainment and you are the one who delivers. It's a win-win.

In The Genre Bundle, we will walk you through all the key elements for you to create a complete novel outline. This will come into play in part 2 of the workbook where you will outline your novel in greater detail. Each time you add an extra layer to your outline you make your novel stronger.

Our motto is *"**plan smart, write easy.**"* So without further ado, let's dive straight in.

The Words Most Frequently Used In Bestselling Book Descriptions

In this section, we will look at which words are most frequently used in bestselling book descriptions. Why have we included this information for you in the workbook? It is so you can start from a solid footing, using words that you know are appropriate for the genre. By using this list as a starting point for the initial idea for your fantasy fiction novel, you know you'll be on to a winner. These books are bestsellers for a reason – they are getting the most search traffic.

You want to tap into the fantasy novel writing formula, using these words below as idea prompts.

We have looked at the top 50 bestselling books in the fantasy fiction genre. We found the most common words used were: (These are taken from the workbook)

WORDS MOST FREQUENTLY USED IN BLURBS:
WORLD, NEW, MAGIC, DEADLY, EMPIRE, MONSTERS, GREAT, SURVIVE, ADVENTURE, KILL, POWERFUL, FAMILY, FIRE, WAR, TIME, ANCIENT, FOUND, KNIGHT, VAMPIRE, KINGS, WORSE, DRAGONS, URBAN, BLOOD, QUESTIONS, OPPORTUNITY, WILD, MIDNIGHT, EPIC, STONES, KINGDOM, ARMY, DEAD, BAD GUYS, MYSTERIOUS, HIDDEN, WEREWOLVES, ASSASSIN, DEATH, ELVES, CENTURIES, DOOM, RULED, REVEALED, FALL, CITY, THREATS

These words cannot fail to get your creative juices flowing. They root you in the mindset correct for fantasy writing. Using this list, you should start to jot down what images and thoughts are evoked. Now try and join some words together. You will end up with five or six strong, evocative words which will set your idea off in your head.

As you can see from the workbook example, we chose:

THE WORDS I PICKED TO USE:

MAGIC, EMPIRE, ADVENTURE, MIDNIGHT, HIDDEN CENTURIES, REVEALED, DEATH, THREATS

MY EXAMPLE:
A YOUNG GIRL DISCOVERS SHE IS A MEMBER OF A CULT IN THE FOREST. SHE IS THE ONLY ONE WHO POSSESSES THE MAGIC TO OVERTURN THE LEADERS AS THEY FIGHT TO EXPAND THEIR EMPIRES AND DESTROY EVERYTHING IN THEIR PATH. UNABLE TO LEAVE, THIS GIRL EMBARKS ON AN EPIC ADVENTURE AT MIDNIGHT. SOON AFTER, IT IS REVEALED THE FURTHER AWAY SHE GETS FROM THE CULT, THE MORE POWERFUL SHE BECOMES. SHE LEARNS ABOUT THE DARK HIDDEN HISTORY OF THIS CULT THAT GOES BACK CENTURIES. WHEN WORD GETS OUT SHE MAY LEAVE SHE FACES DEATH THREATS.

I came up with this example in minutes. The possibilities are endless.

Our example now gives us:

- A main character (protagonist)
- A predicament being faced by the protagonist
- A complication in the story to be solved
- An idea of what the conflict might be between the protagonist and the antagonist/cult

This information has come from words most frequently used in best-selling book descriptions. We're off and running now, we have our idea.

It is such a simple system of generating ideas by looking at what is already selling. We're not trying to reinvent the wheel here. We want to give the readers what they want, with our new, fresh spin on things.

In the workbook, you will see a 'your turn' section. Write down your own choice of words here from the list provided.

Once you have got your idea down you can start to get excited. You are now on your way to creating a summary of a novel that will become the basis of your winning novel outline.

Let's move on to the next element of the summary, **Character Names And Roles**.

Character Names And Roles

One of the most debated parts of planning a novel is 'how many characters will I need?' The simple answer is there is no rule. You can have as many characters as you need to build a compelling narrative. Some novels have fewer than others, and some have so many it's difficult to remember them all.

The most important thing to remember is that you must at least have the basic six characters:

- A hero (the main protagonist)
- A villain (the main antagonist)
- An ally to the hero
- An ally to the villain
- Someone for the hero to save from the villain
- A confidante to the hero

As long as you have these six characters, you will be able to construct a narrative that will support your plot.

Each character must perform some kind of function in the story. Even if they are only present in your story for a line, paragraph or whole chapter. They must achieve a goal, or provide a service to the main character. The effort you go to in describing a character must equate to the level of importance you give to their role in the story.

If you go into great detail about the wizard who gives the magic potion to the main character then give that same wizard enough to do in the story to justify this level of detail. Unless you are deliberately being subtle. Is your wizard going to reappear later in the narrative in a plot twist?

In the workbook, we have started you off with the most common names found in the top 50 bestselling fantasy novels.

CHARACTER NAMES:

ARIA, LUNA, NOVA, ORION, EMBER, WILLOW, ROWAN, FREYJA, CADEN, JASPER, ADRIA, NIAMH, ROHAN, LARK, ZEPHYR, SABLE, MERRICK, FAE, PHOENIX, GWEN

There are lots to choose from here. If you don't like the sound of any of them, or want a greater choice, you can google 'name generators' which will give you more. With fantasy fiction writing, you can really let your imagination run wild with names as they don't have to be ones we recognise in real life.

We have also added a list of roles for your characters:

CHARACTER ROLES:

COMPANION, GOD, GODDESS, MAGICIAN, SORCERER, WARRIOR, MEDIC, HEALER, SOLDIER, THIEF, CRIMINAL, SCHOLER, MERCHANT, LEADER, SHAPESHIFTER, HUNTER, ASSASSIN, TIME TRAVELLER, MIND READER, ILLUSIONIST, STUDENT

Again, the point of including these in the workbook is to show you what the top 50 bestsellers are including. You want to hit the right notes and give the readers what they want. Aim to give them what they expect and what they've come to recognise as genre-specific in your writing.

Finding the right name for a character is a huge stumbling block for writers, as our research has shown. So, here you have a long list of options, and a method of finding more if none of the names in the list hit the mark for you. Please do feel free to use your own ideas here. At the end of the day it is your novel. What we want to achieve with this workbook is to get your ideas flowing. We don't want to restrict you with a finite amount of ideas. Our list is to get you started.

One tip with using names in a story is to ensure they sound different to stop the reader getting confused. An example could be 'John' 'Joan' and 'Jim' all in the same scene. This may make your reader have to work hard differentiate and put them off reading your story.

Here is our pretend example now, using some of the names from the list in the workbook.

A HERO - ARIA (A MAGICIAN)
A VILLAIN - ROHAN (LEADER)
AN ALLY TO THE HERO - CADEN (A STUDENT)
AN ALLY TO THE VILLAIN - ZEPHYR (CRIMINAL)
SOMEONE FOR THE HERO TO SAVE FROM THE VILLAIN - (FAE - HEALER)
A CONFIDANTE TO THE HERO - LUNA (GODDESS)

Our example is starting to build. Use the workbook to fill in your own. Make sure you include the "big six" as a bare minimum.

Let's move on now to the next section, **Events.**

Events

Every novel has a main event that kicks off the action or an event that is at the centre of the narrative. We have looked at the top 50 bestselling fantasy fiction books and listed all the events that happen in them. This is to give you an extensive list to cherry-pick your favourites from. You can then construct your narrative around them.

Events can lead to a plot twist or turning point in the novel, so these can give us rich food for thought.

They can be:

- Exciting events
- Plot twist devices
- 'Boring-but necessary-for-the-narrative' events
- Events that turn the story on its head

They can also provoke a range of different emotions.

> **EVENTS:**
> WAR, MURDER, JOURNEY, QUEST, DISCOVERY, REBELLION, JOURNEY, CONFRONTATION, REVELATION, BETRAYAL, RESOLUTION, BATTLE, DISASTER, FORBIDDEN LOVE, TOURNAMENT, CONTEST, RESCUE, TRANSFORMATION, SHOWDOWN, INVESTIGATION, VICTORY

As you can see there is a huge range of possibilities there to get your thoughts racing. These ideas are taken from the workbook.

For the idea we are building in the workbook to show you how it's done we have chosen the event to be a rescue operation. This gives the main character, Aria the opportunity to meet Fae and escape the cult that is the main threat in the story.

Now, pick the events that give you the most scope to develop into an intriguing plot line.

What if your fantasy story involved a rebellion? Or a battle to end all battles? You can send your story off in so many directions and off on so many tangents.

There are so many ways our narrative can go off on its own path and surprise us as writers too!

Whatever you choose, your primary focus should be, "will this benefit the reader?" We want them to enjoy the rollercoaster ride, remember?

Next up, we will look at **Locations** and where our narrative should take place.

Locations

Locations are similar in some ways to events, in that they define where the main action is due to take place. You can choose as many as fit your plot development, and mix them up where you see fit. Remember, you should have a couple of main places so you can anchor your reader.

> **LOCATIONS:**
> FOREST, SPACE, KINGDOM, EMPIRE, WILDERNESS, HIDDEN CITY, UNDERGROUND, MYSTERIOUS ISLAND, COASTAL TOWN, CASTLE, FORTRESS, MYSTICAL MOUNTAIN, CAVE, SCHOOL, TOWN, VILLAGE

If the fantasy in the alternate world is the main plot line then the alternate world will be your central location.

Ensure that you keep the description of this main location exact in every detail each time. Otherwise you will do the opposite of anchoring your reader. You will disorientate them as they will begin to picture this location as they read your story. If your main character lives in a treehouse in an enchanted forest, make sure the branches are on the same side of the trees, and the details are described the same way. Make sure all elements are in the same place each time.

For our workbook example our main location is a forest where the cast of characters are trying to escape from a murderous cult who want to destroy everything in their path. We want this location to intrigue the reader so therefore we will include as much supplementary details as possible, such as descriptions of the magical elements and the dark spiritual nature of the cult leaders.

The locations we have chosen for our story are:

- Forest
- Empire
- Mystical mountain

This is what we have build so far for our example:

WHAT DO WE HAVE NOW?...

After defeating Rohan and his cult, Aria and Caden are hailed as heroes by the rebels and the people of the forest. But they soon discover that their victory was only the beginning of a much larger conflict. The cult's empire is in fact led by the shadowy figure known as the Emperor, who has never been seen but is determined to reclaim the forest, consume its powers, and crush all resistance.

As the rebels prepare for war, Aria and Caden are approached by a group of powerful sorcerers who offer to teach them the ancient magic of the mystical mountain. The mountain is said to be home to the spirits of the earth, who possess the power to control the elements and bend reality itself. It is here where their powers will combine to defeat the Emperor and the cult once and for all.

Determined to learn as much as they can and gain the upper hand against the empire, Aria and Caden journey to the mountain and begin their training. But as they delve deeper into the secrets of the mountain, they uncover a shocking truth: the Emperor is not who they thought he was, and the true source of his power is far more sinister than anyone could have imagined.

Just when all hope seems lost, Aria and Caden are visited by Luna, the goddess of the moon. Luna reveals to them that she has been watching over them since the beginning of their journey and that she has a special role for them to play in the war against the Emperor.

She gives them the secrets of the ancient magic of the moon, which is the only magic powerful enough to defeat the Emperor and his dark powers.

With the help of Luna's magic, Aria and Caden lead the rebels into battle against the Emperor and his minions.

In a final showdown, they confront the Emperor and use the power of the moon to defeat him and his dark magic.

The war ends in victory

Next, we will look at **Titles** for your fantasy fiction novel, and the importance of choosing the right subtitle.

Titles And Subtitles

Thinking of a title for your epic novel is one of the hardest parts of novel writing. How do you encapsulate a 90,000-word idea into one sentence?

Our method will make the process easier for you. In the workbook, we give you a range of fantasy fiction novel titles that are currently on sale. From the words in these existing titles, you can piece together a title for yourself. Sounds simple, and it is. Any job is simpler when you have a range of tools with which to do it. It's quite complicated to chop down a tree, but much easier if you have an axe, and a doddle if you have a chainsaw. Equip yourself with knowledge and a kitbag of ideas and anything is doable.

What we're NOT encouraging you to do is copy a title. Even though titles are not copyrightable, it is not ok to copy word-for-word a title that is currently used. The only exception to this is if your title option is ubiquitous enough for this not to be a big deal. Copying a title like 'The Room', "The Passion" or "The House" may seem acceptable, but it's not an intriguing title. Especially when you consider the other options available.

If you intend to piggyback on the success of JK Rowling or JRR Tolkien by using a title they've used, it's not a good idea. When your reader realises the book they've found is NOT the right one, they will ignore your book like white noise. They will add the Rowling or Tolkien book to their basket instead. If you are a reader, judge yourself by your own buying behaviour. Would YOU, as a reader, like an author choosing an identical title to a bestseller to trick you into buying their book? I would be more annoyed by this and would avoid their book in protest at their surreptitious attempt to deceive me.

The moral of the story is "emulate, but don't copy". Get the tone right with the words you choose, sum up the book and the main essence of it, and choose your title based on that. If your book is good enough, and you edit/proofread (more on that later) to the highest standard, then your book, like cream, will rise to the top on its own merit. Not through piggybacking another.

Your title should ask questions of the reader that they need to find the answers to – which they will do by reading your book.

For example, our debut novel was titled, **'Meet Me at 10'** so straight away the reader would be thinking, "meet who at ten? And why?" "Ten am or ten pm?" They are also intrigued about what would happen if these two didn't meet at 10. What are the consequences? If there are consequences, who will suffer them?

So straight off the bat, there are mysteries for the reader to solve. Psychologically speaking, the human brain cannot cope with not solving problems. We are, by nature, curious beings. We seek answers to questions. So posing one in your title is a perfect way of piquing the book buyer's interest.

So now we have a starting point for our title – does it provoke questions? The next thing to consider is what your readers like in the fantasy fiction genre. They like familiarity. They like to see titles that look like they fit in this genre, in length too. Often, fantasy fiction novels have 3-4 words in their title. We saw this from our research into the top 50 bestsellers.

Now what you will need is a vocabulary of words to piece together your winning title.

> **TITLES:**
> DEADLY KNIGHT, FIRE AND BLOOD, RED RISING, RISE OF THE GIANTS, DARK TIDE RISING, NIGHT GODDESS, WRATH OF THE GODDESS, A DRAGONS CHAINS, SECRET OF THE YELLOW MOON, THE GAME OF THRONES, LADY OF THE LAKE, THE EYE OF THE WORLD, HE WHO FIGHTS WITH MONSTERS, BLOOD OF ELVES, KNIFE OF DREAMS, THE TWO TOWERS, THE CROWN OF SWORDS, THE PATH OF DAGGERS, THE DRAGON REBORN

This is where the list in the workbook (pictured above) will help to inspire you and get your ideas flowing. All the titles in the top 50 bestsellers make up this list. So now you can mix and match to your hearts' content, to find the title that best sums up your work. See what words generate images in your head, and what side plots they drum up so you can add them to your story. Have fun with it.

You will by now, have your bare-bones outline in your head. What would be a good, thought-provoking, question-asking title for it? Even if it is a working title, for now, get one down.

The ideas we came up with when we looked at the list in the workbook were as follows:

GODDESS OF THE MOON
THE BLOOD OF THE WORLD
THE SECRET RISING
WRATH OF THE DAGGERS
SMALL GIANTS RISING

We put together these titles using words that intrigued us – and as a title, they ask questions of the reader. 'Where does the blood come from?' and 'What secret is rising?' In a nutshell, pick a few words, put them together and see where it takes you. Great news for the "pantsers" amongst us.

The one that piqued our interest the most on reflection was **'Goddess Of The Moon'** 'What moon?' 'Who is the Goddess?' So already we have succeeded in our task of getting the reader to ask questions.

When we create our book cover with this title, it will fit on the shelf with the other bestsellers. This is because we have followed the pattern the top 50 bestsellers use. You may be thinking, "ok, but this isn't rocket science' and that's fine. This is a guidebook intended to remind you to consider the elements of the genre that beforehand you might not have seen the importance of doing. So, if it's given you at least a few new things to think about then it's done its job.

S.E.O - Search Engine Optimisation

The next part we have to add to our title is a subtitle. There are a few reasons to do this. One is, it adds more detail to the title to reinforce the type of book it is and to further entice the buyer to 'add to cart.' There is no doubt that it is the title of the book that will entice the reader. But did you know that it is the subtitle that helps you to get found in online searches? Worded well, your subtitle forms the basis of what the buyer is typing into a search box.

For example, a reader may type this into a search box, as this is what they are looking for:

If you reverse engineer this and put words like this in your subtitle, it will be your book that shows up!

SEO stands for 'search engine optimisation'. You want to add into your subtitle the words that are getting searched for the most by readers in your genre. This helps your book to appear in their search results.

Optimising your book listing is well worth spending time on. It will help you to show up in search results and put you well on your way to making sales.

For our example novel, **'Goddess Of The Moon**,' we used the words, *'A Fantasy Adventure Novel For Young Adults'* in our subtitle. As we can see from the search bar example above, this is quite a common search term. So putting it into our subtitle will ensure our book gets found in the search results. It might not be at the top, but it will feature on that page somewhere, which is a great start.

Below is a list of search terms that rated high in our research conducted using Publisher Rocket.

**FANTASY ADVENTURE FICTION
HISTORICAL FANTASY FICTION
FANTASY NOVEL FOR ADULTS
FANTASY YOUNG ADULT
FANTASY NOVEL FOR KIDS 9-12
FANTASY BOOK FOR TEENS
FANTASY ADVENTURE BOOK
FANTASY ROMANCE BOOK**

Publisher Rocket is excellent as a data scraper tool to help you to create your subtitles. Use the list provided above if you want a quicker more convenient way to create your subtitle.

If you were to type into a search box on an online book store page 'historical fiction set in the deep south' then our novel **'Meet Me at 10'** will show up on the first page.

This is because those words are in our subtitle and our backend keywords. Keywords are what you add when you upload your book to an online selling platform. These keywords lead the reader to your book. It is the algorithm's way of showing our book is a good fit for the buyer. The selling platform does this because it means there is more chance of a sale. Good news for them too, as they get a cut of the profits.

One thing you must avoid though is something called 'keyword stuffing'. This is where you overload your description with too many keywords. It will look clunky and obvious that you've tried to do that. For example, if we overstuffed our subtitle for **'Goddess Of The Moon'** where it read, *fantasy adventure and historical romance for* *teens'* together, it would be overkill. You could use some of these extra words in your book description. All used at the time in a subtitle, it would take up a lot of space on your cover.

You've got to think, what would your reader type into the search bar? If you're not sure about that, think of your own 'buying behaviour.' What would you type into a search bar? You might type in, 'fantasy adventure' or 'fantasy romance'. Put yourself in your reader's position and you're onto a winner – or ask them!

Be subtle, be specific, and above all, consider what your target audience may type into a search bar. Then reverse engineer that and pick words for your subtitle that match the type of book it is that you've written. Then you are giving your book the best possible chance of appearing in search results. That all-important sale will be within your reach.

Next, we will look at the **Do's And Don't's Of The Genre.** These are so important to consider. You don't want to fall into the trap of making your writing cliched, old hat and predictable.

Do's And Don't's Of The Genre

For this section of the workbook, we have gone through Amazon's top 50 bestselling fantasy fiction novels again. We have noted down all the positive and negative comments from the reviews of these books. These comments highlight what readers are loving – and hating – about the books they have read and reviewed.

This section intends to help you avoid these pitfalls from the start. We want you to focus your writing on hitting the positives the readers are commenting on. If you do this then you are near-on guaranteeing success with your novel. You will be ticking all the right boxes, and not annoying your target audience.

Also, you don't want to receive a note back from your editor saying you have to rewrite huge chunks. If you don't give your target audience what it asks for, then your book may receive the dreaded one-star review. This will kill your sales. The reviewer may even go into a long diatribe on why readers should avoid your novel. Reviewers can be brutal and uncaring for the feelings of the author.

This part of the workbook is crucial information. You want to hit the right note with your target audience from the first book you write.

> **DO'S**
> - THE CONCEPTS, THE IDEAS AND THE EXECUTION OF THE BOOKS IS NEAR FLAWLESS.
> - EASY TO READ.
> - VERY CLEVER WRITING.
> - WELL-DEVELOPED CHARACTERS.
> - DIFFERENT FROM MY USUAL READS.
> - GREAT CHARACTERS.
> - FANTASTIC ENDING.
> - GRIPPING STORY.
> - INTERESTING SCENES AND WORLD-BUILDING WITH GOOD CHARACTERS.

The first 'do' is that the concepts, ideas and the execution of the books is near flawless. How good of a review would that be for your book? This is exactly the standard you should be setting for yourself with your writing.

Make your readers love the 'clever writing' and the 'well-developed characters.' Don't end on a flat resolution. Give them a 'gripping story' and 'fantastic ending' to justify the length of time they have spent reading your book.

Reviewers are also saying they want easy-to-read, interesting scenes in your book. Give them plot twists, exciting outcomes and some clever dialogue as well.

Let's take a moment to look at the key 'don't's' that readers are highlighting:

DON'TS
- CRINGE-WORTHY SILLY.
- POORLY TOLD IDEA.
- STOPPED READING AFTER CHAPTER 2.
- THE WRITER REALLY SHOULD HAVE GOTTEN SOMEONE TO READ THIS BOOK BEFORE SENDING OUT.
- I COULDN'T FINISH IT.
- A STRING OF CLICHES.
- UNLIKEABLE CHARACTERS.
- TOO MUCH LIKE HARD WORK.
- RIDICULOUSLY LONG PASSAGES.
- RIDICULOUS METAPHORS AND SIMILES.
- SILLY CHARACTER NAMES.
- CONFUSING.
- HARD TO FOLLOW.

One of the main gripes readers in this genre had was the book having *'a poorly told idea'*. This is one of our main gripes too! Too many TV shows/films we've watched recently have left us unsatisfied by an illogical or weak idea. Don't let your book be the same. The reader will never read a single thing you write again if you blow it on the first book.

Here are some more things your readers *don't* want:

DON'T'S

Book reviews of fantasy fiction novels generally do not want the following things:

- Lack of world-building: **Fantasy fiction relies heavily on world-building, and readers often expect to be fully immersed in a detailed and believable world. If the world-building is weak or confusing, it can be a major turn-off for reviewers.**

- Flat or uninteresting characters: **In any genre, well-developed and compelling characters are crucial to a successful book. If the characters in a fantasy fiction novel are shallow or uninteresting, reviewers may be turned off.**

- Lack of plot or conflict: **A good fantasy fiction novel should have a clear and compelling plot that keeps readers engaged from beginning to end. If the plot is weak or lacks conflict, reviewers may be disappointed.**

- Poor writing quality: **While fantasy fiction often includes complex world-building and complex characters, the writing itself should still be well-crafted and engaging. Poor writing quality can be a major turn-off for reviewers.**

- Clichéd or unoriginal ideas: **While many fantasy fiction novels draw on common themes and tropes, reviewers generally want to see something fresh and unique in the story. If a book feels overly familiar or unoriginal, reviewers may be less likely to enjoy it.**

Going through this list of what to do/not do will enhance your writing. It will give you an understanding of what current readers are reflecting on in their reviews. Be one step ahead and give them what they want.

On that note, it is time to look at overused **Tropes** in fantasy fiction, and character **Stereotypes** to avoid. This will be the focus of our next section.

Fantasy Tropes And Stereotypes

What is a trope?

A trope is an overused convention within a particular genre. It refers to any element that is so common in a genre that readers recognise it. They feel comfortable that they know what to expect from the book.

For example: **the main character is in a life-or-death battle with a mystical force.**

So, we've established that a trope helps readers establish the set elements of a genre. That should be a good thing, right? Well, yes. But overusing them to where they make the genre stale and predictable then becomes bad for a writer. What we need to do is refresh the clichés. Try to do something different in your narrative. Aim to avoid the most overused tropes. You will turn your reader off if they feel they are reading a book with the "same old, same old" conventions in it.

One example trope we talk about in the workbook is:

Trope 1: The chosen one

This is a common trope in fantasy fiction where a character is chosen by fate or prophecy to fulfil a special destiny or quest.

This character is often a person who is unexpectedly thrust into a position of great responsibility and must learn to harness their untapped potential in order to save the day.

We see this time and time again, so much so that it has become dull and predictable. Why not make 'the chosen one' a character who is an unlikely hero? This could make the character a more relatable and down-to-earth hero for readers to root for.

Trope 2: The magical world is hidden from the mortal world

Many fantasy stories feature a magical world that is hidden from the mortal world, either through spells or by being located in a different realm or dimension. This magical world is often filled with fantastic creatures and magical beings and may be threatened by some great evil or conflict that the protagonist must help to defeat.

Another trope example we explore in the workbook is the one where the magical world is hidden from the mortal world. Again, a bit boring and predictable, so why not make magic part of everyday life from the get-go. Make magic accepted and integral to life, where characters use magic for normal, humdrum daily activities, and magical creatures appearing as standard. This will help you to create a more immersive and integrated world where magic is not something mysterious and unknown, but rather a natural part of the world.

Trope 3: The mentor or wise old man:

In many fantasy stories, the protagonist is aided by a mentor or wise old man who helps them to understand their powers or abilities and guides them on their quest. This character is often a wise and experienced figure who has a deep understanding of the magical world and is able to offer valuable guidance and insight to the protagonist.

One more trope we cover in the workbook is the age-old trope of "the mentor or wise old man." What if we made the wise old man a wise old *woman*? O even a wise *young* woman/man? That could give us a new spin on things. Rarely do we see this, so why not explore this option for your own narrative? Again, this is a call to all the "pantsers" out there; let's walk down this path and see where it takes us.

Already by refreshing the old tropes, we can see how many avenues of opportunity open up to us. Take the old idea, and flip it around to see what it offers up. You may uncover a nugget of pure gold there, one that knocks that writer's block right out of the park!

What is a stereotype?

A stereotype is a fixed set of characteristics or ideals that a group of people agree represents a specific type of person.

THE SUCCESSFUL BUSINESSMAN,
THE HARASSED SINGLE MOTHER,
THE HARDNOSED SPINSTER
THE BRAINY VILLAIN HELL-BENT ON TAKING OVER THE WORLD.

Cliched characteristics form the basis of stereotypes. Once readers are aware of them, they begin to expect certain actions from the characters.

You will bore your reader with a character displaying stereotypical traits. Your predictable character will become a waste of words in your novel. Worse still, your reader won't forgive you for it. Especially if they read a lot of fantasy fiction novels, it will put them off straight away. Give your character an unfamiliar, rarely-used, trait. Even if they are a rich and powerful businessman. Make him a toy collector in his spare time. Create the stalker-type spinster donating to children's charities in secret.

There is so much you can do to refresh the tropes and stereotypes we come to see a lot in fantasy fiction novels. It takes a little creativity and fleshing out of your characters. But we will come to that later.

Here is a recap of what we have build to far for **'Goddess Of The Moon'**:

GODDESS OF THE MOON: LUNA'S GUIDE TO ARIA'S ESCAPE
A FANTASY ADVENTURE NOVEL FOR YOUNG ADULTS

WHEN ARIA DISCOVERS THAT SHE IS A MEMBER OF A SINISTER CULT DEEP IN THE FOREST, SHE KNOWS SHE MUST ESCAPE BEFORE IT'S TOO LATE. THE CULT, LED BY THE RUTHLESS ROHAN, WILL STOP AT NOTHING TO EXPAND HIS EMPIRE AND DESTROY ANYONE WHO STANDS IN HIS WAY. BUT ARIA IS NOT ALONE IN HER QUEST TO OVERTHROW THE LEADERS AND SAVE FAE, A HEALER WHO HAS BEEN TARGETED BY THE CULT'S DARK SPIRITS.

WITH THE HELP OF CADEN, A POWERFUL ALLY SHE MEETS ON HER JOURNEY, ARIA LEARNS ABOUT THE CULT'S DARK HISTORY AND THE KEY TO HER OWN MAGICAL ABILITIES. AS SHE GROWS IN STRENGTH AND COURAGE, SHE BECOMES THE TARGET OF THE CULT'S DEATH THREATS. BUT ARIA REFUSES TO GIVE UP, EVEN WHEN FACED WITH OVERWHELMING ODDS. WITH THE GUIDANCE OF THE GODDESS LUNA, ARIA MUST FIND THE STRENGTH TO ESCAPE THE CULT AND RECLAIM HER FREEDOM ONCE AND FOR ALL.

CAN ARIA AND CADEN OVERCOME THE DANGERS OF THE CULT AND OUTWIT ROHAN AND HIS FOLLOWERS, OR WILL THEY SUCCUMB TO THE THREATS AGAINST THEM?

MY CHARACTERS NAMES/ROLES ARE:

A HERO - ARIA (A MAGICIAN)
A VILLAIN - ROHAN (LEADER)
AN ALLY TO THE HERO - CADEN (A STUDENT)
AN ALLY TO THE VILLAIN - ZEPHYR (CRIMINAL)
SOMEONE FOR THE HERO TO SAVE FROM THE VILLAIN - (FAE - HEALER)
A CONFIDANTE TO THE HERO - LUNA (GODDESS)

Power Words

In this section, we will look at how we can create plot twists in our writing using power words. This is an important part of your planning. It enables you to mix things up a bit in your narrative and surprise your reader. You will knock them off the safe platform your narrative has put them on over the last few chapters.

Power words are strong, emotive words that signify an action or an emotion, such as:

EPIC, ADVENTURE, THRILLING, INTENSE, FAST-PACED, ACTION-PACKED, MYSTERIOUS, BREATHTAKING, POWERFUL, BATTLE, MAGIC, QUEST, CURSE, LEGEND, FIGHT, BATTLE, CONQUER, RESCUE, ESCAPE, JOURNEY, VOYAGE, EXPLORE, TRAVEL, WANDER, TREK, SUMMON, DEFEAT, SHAPE-SHIFT, TELEPORT, HEALING, INVISIBLE, LEVITATE, TRANSFORM, BANISH, HEX, ENCHANT, BLAST, EXPOSE, REVEAL, MANIFEST, OVERCOME, PROTECT, EMPOWER, FOUGHT, FIGHT, DARK, SECRET, DESTINY, CREATURES, POWERS, SWORD, FORBIDDEN, DARKNESS, HERO, SPIRIT, PORTAL, ASSASSIN, WIZARD, WITCH, VILLAIN, TYRANT, DIVIDE, UNRAVEL, DISGUISE, DECIPHER, UNCOVER, UNMASK, CONFRONT, CORRUPT, OVERTHROW, EVOLVE, UNITE, BETRAY, BETRAYAL, CONCEAL

These words carry more meaning and evoke a stronger reaction in the reader. Power words add depth to your writing. The power word examples above (featured in the workbook) are all taken from the book descriptions of the top 50 bestsellers. They are excellent examples for you to scatter throughout your writing.

We will use them to create nail-biting plot twist ideas to get our creative thoughts racing.

Aim to slot about 2-3 power words into your plot twists. If you're heavy-handed with power words you will put off your reader as it looks a bit like you are trying too hard. Writing is all about using standard "blue-brick" words as the building blocks of your prose. You can then throw in some "red brick" power words to mix up the pace and colour of the narrative. This will add depth and strength to your writing.

In our example story, **'Goddess Of The Moon,'** we used the power words:

- Invisible
- Shape-shift
- Forbidden
- Betray

This gave us some rich ideas for developing the following plot twists:

INVISIBLE:

Just when Aria and Caden think they have escaped the cult and are safe, they discover that they have been marked with a powerful curse that makes them invisible to the outside world.

SHAPE-SHIFT:

As Aria and Caden journey deeper into the forest, they are confronted by Rohan's most loyal followers, who are determined to stop them from leaving. In a desperate bid for survival, Aria discovers that she has the ability to shape-shift into different forms, including animals and mythical creatures. She uses this power to evade her pursuers and escape from the cult.

However, Aria's ability to shape-shift comes with a price: each time she uses it, she becomes more and more animalistic, losing touch with her human side. She begins to fear that she may never be able to return to her human form, and that she will be trapped in her animal form forever.

FORBIDDEN:

As Aria and Caden journey deeper into the forest, they come across a group of rebels who are fighting against the cult's reign of terror. The rebels reveal that they have discovered a forbidden magic that could help Aria and Caden defeat Rohan and his followers.

The forbidden magic is a powerful force that has been hidden away for centuries, feared and reviled by all who know of its existence. As they delve deeper into the forbidden magic, they begin to uncover a sinister plot by Rohan and his followers to use the magic for their own gain.

BETRAY:

Aria and Caden are certain that they can trust their ally, Fae, to help them defeat Rohan and his cult. However, as they journey deeper into the forest, they begin to suspect that Fae is hiding something from them. She has set out to betray them all along for her own gain.

These power words give our narrative a clear direction in which to go – and shake up the status quo in the story. What if Aria and Caden were marked with a curse that made them invisible? Or they could shape-shift? That would really set the action up as they would be able to hide from the villains and destroy them from the inside.

So now we have added more intrigue to our narrative by slotting in some interesting power words. It gets the reader exploring possible plot twists in the narrative. It helps them to stay hooked on trying to track the events and the turns in the road. Above all, it cements your reputation of being the writer that cooks up the most epic of plot twists. What reader wouldn't want to rip your next book off the shelf now?

Here is a summary of what we have now with **'Goddess Of The Moon'**:

GODDESS OF THE MOON: LUNA'S GUIDE TO ARIA'S ESCAPE
A FANTASY ADVENTURE NOVEL FOR YOUNG ADULTS

WHEN ARIA DISCOVERS THAT SHE IS A MEMBER OF A SINISTER CULT DEEP IN THE FOREST, SHE KNOWS SHE MUST ESCAPE BEFORE IT'S TOO LATE. THE CULT, LED BY THE RUTHLESS ROHAN, WILL STOP AT NOTHING TO EXPAND HIS EMPIRE AND DESTROY ANYONE WHO STANDS IN HIS WAY. BUT ARIA IS NOT ALONE IN HER QUEST TO OVERTHROW THE LEADERS AND SAVE FAE, A HEALER WHO HAS BEEN TARGETED BY THE CULT'S DARK SPIRITS.

WITH THE HELP OF CADEN, A POWERFUL ALLY SHE MEETS ON HER JOURNEY, ARIA LEARNS ABOUT THE CULT'S DARK HISTORY AND THE KEY TO HER OWN MAGICAL ABILITIES. AS SHE GROWS IN STRENGTH AND COURAGE, SHE BECOMES THE TARGET OF THE CULT'S DEATH THREATS. BUT ARIA REFUSES TO GIVE UP, EVEN WHEN FACED WITH OVERWHELMING ODDS. WITH THE GUIDANCE OF THE GODDESS LUNA, ARIA MUST FIND THE STRENGTH TO ESCAPE THE CULT AND RECLAIM HER FREEDOM ONCE AND FOR ALL.

CAN ARIA AND CADEN OVERCOME THE DANGERS OF THE CULT AND OUTWIT ROHAN AND HIS FOLLOWERS, OR WILL THEY SUCCUMB TO THE THREATS AGAINST THEM?

MY CHARACTERS NAMES/ROLES ARE:

A HERO - ARIA (A MAGICIAN)
A VILLAIN - ROHAN (LEADER)
AN ALLY TO THE HERO - CADEN (A STUDENT)
AN ALLY TO THE VILLAIN - ZEPHYR (CRIMINAL)
SOMEONE FOR THE HERO TO SAVE FROM THE VILLAIN - (FAE - HEALER)
A CONFIDANTE TO THE HERO - LUNA (GODDESS)

PLOT TWISTS CREATED BY THE POWER WORDS I HAVE CHOSEN:

JUST WHEN ARIA AND CADEN THINK THEY HAVE ESCAPED THE CULT AND ARE SAFE, THEY DISCOVER THAT THEY HAVE BEEN MARKED WITH A POWERFUL CURSE THAT MAKES THEM INVISIBLE TO THE OUTSIDE WORLD. ARIA CAN SHAPE-SHIFT TO ESCAPE, BUT CADEN CAN'T

In the next section, we will look at **More Plot Twists To Add To Your Ending**. This will further develop your plot twist ideas so that we can set them up so they are believable. Let's do them justice, eh?

More Plot Twists To Add To Your Ending

If there's one thing that's imperative to get right in novel writing, no matter what genre you write in, it's the ending. It's amazing the number of times we've watched a film/TV series, or read a book with a super unsatisfying ending. We could fill a novel itself with them. The ending is the most important part of your novel. It is the part where all the strands you have woven come together and the reader gets what's known as the 'pay-off. This is the reward for all their hard work reading your book. It rewards their diligence in trying to solve your mysteries.

If you read any one-star book review you will find a comment mentioning the ending as being a total let-down. No one has 4-5 hours to waste reading an unsatisfying book. It is the one thing that will be the topic of conversation when they talk about it afterwards. If your ending is rubbish then the reviewer will add in a "but" halfway through their review. Our mission in this section is to help you to avoid your ending being the topic of the "but" sentence.

From a writing perspective, we usually have a fair idea of how we want our ending to go. Many writers even have their endings planned out in their heads. It is sometimes the seed idea of the novel. What they do is work backwards and construct the plot and narrative around it. What we want to help you with is getting there in a way that makes the plot twist leading to the ending believable.

Writers often say: "I have a great idea for an ending, but don't know how to lay the breadcrumbs to get the readers there." What we offer them is the following advice:

- Foreshadow your ending at the beginning
- Revisit in the middle
- Wallop it in at the end

In this part of the workbook, we will help you to think up how you get from the beginning to the middle and then to the end. Later on in the workbook, in the planning pages, we will break down each part further, scene by scene.

To keep the reader hooked, writers need to take each act of the story and think "what could be the worst thing to happen at the end?" We will use our example story, **'Goddess Of The Moon'** to further explain how we do this.

We have thought up three "worst things" for the story:

1. CADEN is killed.

2. ARIA is betrayed by everybody she trusts apart from the GODDESS.

3. ARIA is defeated and rejoins the cult.

The first one would be quite strong, as Caden being killed would be heartbreaking for Aria, and the reader. This one feels like it has the most scope to elaborate on.

ACT 3
ENDING

> **CADEN is killed**

The Beginning

To make sure our readers don't guess this plot twist, we need to set up the breadcrumbs from the beginning. We need to set up the complete opposite of option 1 from the start. This is to make the lead-up to the ending as devastating as possible. We have to think, about what would impact the audience the most. What would pull on the heartstrings the most?

ACT 1
BEGINNING

> **CADEN and ARIA are very close and work together**

How about we have both Aria and Caden working together to overthrow the cult that is destroying their world.

To set up a satisfying ending, we need to raise the stakes for Aria and Caden.

The Middle

We are laying the groundwork here for the middle section of the story. This is the part where we develop the storyline and change the mood. We do this so that your big plot twist reveal in the final act is believable and effective.

ACT 2
MIDDLE

> **CADEN gets discovered helping ARIA**

During this middle section, we will see Caden being discovered as the person helping Aria to infiltrate the cult and learn their secrets. This puts Caden at a vey high risk of being killed for this betrayal. Here would be an excellent place to drop in a devastating plot twist - even fantasy fiction readers don't have it easy!

FURTHER PLOT TWIST

> ▶ **ARIA can shape-shift to escape but CADEN can't**

So Aria can shape-shift but Caden can't? Is this the reason he gets killed? This would be especially tragic so is a great option for a plot twist to keep the reader on the edge of their seat. Adding drama in at every turn is a key aspect of fantasy fiction writing, as the reader wants to feel the ups and downs of an exciting fantasy novel, hoping that all the bumps in the road will be ironed out by the end.

This is all well and good, and we will deliver this in our writing as fantasy fiction authors - but the reader will go through hell first! Where's the fun in "straightforward," eh?

Characters Part 2 - Develop Them Further

We need our characters to be even more likeable or relatable and a bit more 3D. This is something that appeared in the readers' comments in the do's/don't's section. On page 64 of the workbook you will find an extensive, but not exhaustive, list of character traits. You can use this list to flesh out the personalities of your characters. Some are positive traits and some are negative. We don't want our characters to be perfect, as this is unrealistic.

Let's take a closer look at the protagonist in our example book, **'Goddess Of The Moon'**

THE MAIN CHARACTER (PROTAGONIST)

NAME: ARIA (MAGICIAN)

POSITIVE TRAITS: BRAVE, ACTIVE, STRONG, CLEVER

NEGATIVE TRAITS: RUDE, IMPULSIVE, VENGEFUL

Aria is a brave, active, strong and clever person, whose main intention is to take down the cult trying to wipe out her people. In this aim, she shows she is a noble and courageous character, one that the reader will be rooting for, to overcome the evil with her powers of good.

We can utilise her negative traits in her overall character arc here. Aria is rude, impulsive and vengeful, which could prove to be her downfall if she gets embroiled in a fight to the death with her sworn enemy, Rohan.

Let's take our 'ally,' Caden next.

THE ALLY

NAME: CADEN (A STUDENT)

POSITIVE TRAITS: HONEST, OPTIMISTIC, CONFIDENT

NEGATIVE TRAITS: TALKATIVE, MESSY, STUBBORN

Caden is honest, optimistic and confident. These are great traits when your role in a fantasy fiction story is the main 'helper' to the protagonist. Caden will act as confidante and counsel also to Aria, all whilst falling in love with her, making the ending even more tragic. His negative traits are that he is talkative, messy and stubborn, which could come int play near the end when his demise occurs.

Fill in positive and negative character traits for all your main players in your novel. This will give you a clear idea of how you want the dynamic between them to develop as the story develops.

Internal And External Goals

Having a sense of your character's internal and external goals allows you to understand them. Especially when it comes to their motivations for how they behave in the narrative.

Internal goals

In this section of the workbook, we explain what an internal goal is. An internal goal hides beneath the surface of your character. They do not share this goal with other characters. It acts as their motivation for everything they do – their end goal for what they want to achieve in life. Inner conflict is created when there is a discord between internal purpose and external goal achievement. In short, the inner goal cannot be achieved unless the external goal is. For example, if the inner goal is pride in oneself then the external goal of scoring the winning goal in the cup final will achieve this. If they miss the penalty, the inner goal is not achieved.

In your writing, you want to try where possible to "show, don't tell". This method adds much more interest to your writing. The following example will highlight this.

The man was angry

vs

The man paced the floor, his fists clenched, his eyes narrowed. He clamped his lips together until they felt numb. The blood boiled in his veins.

The second example paints a visceral picture of the man's emotions. It describes (shows) how he would act if he was feeling angry. Describing the emotion makes it easier to picture when there is more to imagine. Sometimes 'tell' has its place in the narrative, but it is much juicier when you use 'show' in your descriptions.

Let's look at the example we set out in the workbook

For example:

Your character is due to attend a party. They are timid, but their internal goal is to be more confident. Unfortunately, they stumble over their words during a speech they have given before.

Your plot events must show how the character evolves. They will now achieve their internal goal of overcoming their shyness.

We must show in the narrative how the character will overcome this shyness so they can achieve their inner goal. There needs to be a shift in the story that puts the character in a position where they can learn confidence. They then, in time, can make that speech at the party. There will no doubt be successes and failures along the way, but every story needs conflict.

List of internal goals for your characters:

- To overcome personal insecurities and self-doubt
- To find and establish their own identity and sense of self
- To make amends with their past and resolve any

lingering issues or traumas
- To find and pursue their passions and dreams
- To heal and repair damaged relationships with loved ones
- To overcome personal flaws and become a better person
- To find and maintain inner peace and happiness
- To achieve personal growth and self-improvement
- To find and achieve success in their career or chosen field
- To find and maintain a healthy, fulfilling romantic relationship

External goals

An external goal is what the outside world can see. It's the achievement that quantifies the success of the hero. Does the hero get the girl in the end? Do the two main characters walk off into the sunset together at the end? The external conflict is generated by all the pitfalls that the hero experiences along the way.

We need to think about what struggles your character could be battling on the outside. Is this someone who fought to win the love of their beau? Are there battles to face along the way? How you can use this in your writing is "show, don't tell" how your character acts according to their external goal. This will add a greater depth to your writing.

External goals can help us to devise plot twists, as lots can go wrong along the way to achieving an external goal. For example, your character might have to:

- Escape from prison
- Stop something bad from happening
- Deliver something of value so that something good can happen
- Avoid bad outcomes by retrieving something

External goals can also include gaining status, money, or power from events in the novel, or through others' mistakes and actions. The function of the character's enemy is to thwart the main character in their pursuit of the external goal.

List of external goals for your characters:

- To defeat an enemy or rival
- To save someone or something in danger
- To find and obtain an object or goal
- To protect and defend their loved ones or community
- To expose and stop a crime or injustice
- To succeed in a competition or challenge
- To achieve a position of power or influence
- To accomplish a specific task or mission
- To achieve financial stability and success
- To travel to a new location or achieve a personal adventure

We can develop our main character further, as well as add positive and negative traits, by giving them internal and external goals.

THE MAIN CHARACTER (PROTAGONIST)

NAME: ARIA (A MAGICIAN)

INTERNAL GOAL: TO UNDERSTAND HER TRUE PURPOSE IN LIFE AND WHY SHE IS GROWING STRONGER AWAY FROM THE CULT.

THEY CAN SHOW THIS BY: ASKING QUESTIONS WHEN SHE IS WITH LUNA, AND SEEKING OUT KNOWLEDGE FROM THE ELDERS OF THE FOREST.

THE WORST THING TO HAPPEN HERE WOULD BE: THE ONES WHO CAN PROVIDE ENLIGHTENMENT ARE KILLED OR CAPTURED/SWORN TO SILENCE ON PAIN OF DEATH.

The **internal goal** for Aria is to understand her true purpose in life and why she is growing stronger away from the cult.

Having 'the worst thing that could happen here' in your planning gives you great plot twist ideas. Aria's 'worst case scenario' is that the ones who can provide enlightenment to her are killed or captured/sworn to silence on pain of death.

> **EXTERNAL GOAL:** TO DISCOVER THE HIDDEN HISTORY OF THE CULT AND BRING DOWN ITS LEADERS.
>
> **THEY CAN SHOW THIS BY:** RALLYING TROOPS AND FIGHTING OFF THREATS IN BATTLE. SEEKING KNOWLEDGE FROM LUNA.
>
> **THE WORST THING TO HAPPEN HERE WOULD BE:** BATTLES ARE LOST, LUNA IS DESTROYED BEFORE ARIA LEARNS THE TRUTH.

Aria's **external goal** is to discover the hidden history of the cult and bring down its leaders. She can show this by rallying the troops and fight off threats in battle. She can also seek out knowledge from Luna, the Goddess of the moon.

The worst thing to happen to Aria in the pursuit of this external goal is that the battles are lost, and that Luna is destroyed before Aria can learn the truth.

Have a good think about your own characters and their internal/external goals. This will enable you further to flesh them out and make them into three-dimensional characters. Your reader will feel they can identify with them then.

The last section of Part 1 is where we will put our novel summary together.

The Final Amazing Novel Summary

So here we are – where we will put together the total of all the planning we have done so far. By now, you should have a clear idea of the novel you are about to write.

We have researched and included the words that crop up the most in book descriptions. This will ensure your summary is hitting the right note from the get-go. You should have now:

- A full cast list and their roles with the story identified
- Key locations
- Events we want to incorporate into the action
- Possible plot twists using power words
- A killer plot twist to end on

Now all you need to do is write your novel summary out in full.

There is a 'your turn' page in the workbook with plenty of space to do so. If you run out of space, please take advantage of the free extra 'your turn' pages. you can do this by scanning the QR code in the workbook at the bottom of the 'your turn' page.

In the workbook, you can see how our example, **'Goddess Of The Moon'** has come together. We're going to write this book at some point in the future.

GODDESS OF THE MOON: LUNA'S GUIDE TO ARIA'S ESCAPE
A FANTASY ADVENTURE NOVEL FOR YOUNG ADULTS

WHEN ARIA DISCOVERS THAT SHE IS A MEMBER OF A SINISTER CULT DEEP IN THE FOREST, SHE KNOWS SHE MUST ESCAPE BEFORE IT'S TOO LATE. THE CULT, LED BY THE RUTHLESS ROHAN, WILL STOP AT NOTHING TO EXPAND HIS EMPIRE AND DESTROY ANYONE WHO STANDS IN HIS WAY. BUT ARIA IS NOT ALONE IN HER QUEST TO OVERTHROW THE LEADERS AND SAVE FAE, A HEALER WHO HAS BEEN TARGETED BY THE CULT'S DARK SPIRITS.

WITH THE HELP OF CADEN, A POWERFUL ALLY SHE MEETS ON HER JOURNEY, ARIA LEARNS ABOUT THE CULT'S DARK HISTORY AND THE KEY TO HER OWN MAGICAL ABILITIES. AS SHE GROWS IN STRENGTH AND COURAGE, SHE BECOMES THE TARGET OF THE CULT'S DEATH THREATS. BUT ARIA REFUSES TO GIVE UP, EVEN WHEN FACED WITH OVERWHELMING ODDS. WITH THE GUIDANCE OF THE GODDESS LUNA, ARIA MUST FIND THE STRENGTH TO ESCAPE THE CULT AND RECLAIM HER FREEDOM ONCE AND FOR ALL.

CAN ARIA AND CADEN OVERCOME THE DANGERS OF THE CULT AND OUTWIT ROHAN AND HIS FOLLOWERS, OR WILL THEY SUCCUMB TO THE THREATS AGAINST THEM?

MY CHARACTERS NAMES/ROLES ARE:

A HERO - ARIA (A MAGICIAN)
A VILLAIN - ROHAN (LEADER)
AN ALLY TO THE HERO - CADEN (A STUDENT)
AN ALLY TO THE VILLAIN - ZEPHYR (CRIMINAL)
SOMEONE FOR THE HERO TO SAVE FROM THE VILLAIN - (FAE - HEALER)
A CONFIDANTE TO THE HERO - LUNA (GODDESS)

PLOT TWISTS CREATED BY THE POWER WORDS I HAVE CHOSEN:

JUST WHEN ARIA AND CADEN THINK THEY HAVE ESCAPED THE CULT AND ARE SAFE, THEY DISCOVER THAT THEY HAVE BEEN MARKED WITH A POWERFUL CURSE THAT MAKES THEM INVISIBLE TO THE OUTSIDE WORLD. ARIA CAN SHAPE-SHIFT TO ESCAPE, BUT CADEN CAN'T

ENDING USING A KILLER PLOT TWIST:

CADEN IS KILLED.

With your summary, don't edit anything at this point. Let your creative juices flow and don't be afraid to change or tweak your ideas even at this stage. Remember, this is your novel and your ideas will flow throughout this planning stage. This workbook gives lots of opportunities to change your thoughts at any time. You can see how the narrative is developing and where it is taking you. Above all, avoiding the dreaded writer's block - and plot hole - is the main thing this workbook achieves.

Whichever way you roll - 'plotter' or 'pantser' - our workbook gives you the best of both sides. Who knows, even the most ardent plotter may see the merits of flying by the seat of their pants at times. Or even the most adamant "pantser" may appreciate a small breadcrumb trail through their story to follow.

Whatever way gets you writing, it can't be all bad – can it? Go on, plotters – live a little. And pantsers? I won't tell anyone if you secretly plan.

Let's focus on getting some words on the page, eh?

PART II

The Complete Plan: Your Novel Outline

Why Three Acts And Ten Chapters?

In this section of the workbook, you will find a comprehensive structure to help you to plan your novel.

The Three-Act Structure

The three-act structure is the most common way to structure a book. It divides the story into three parts: the beginning, middle and end.

The **first act** introduces the main characters and sets the stage for the rest of the story. The **second act** is the middle part of the story and is where the main conflict or problem is introduced and the characters start working towards resolving it. The **third act** is the final part of the story and is where the main conflict is resolved and the story comes to a close.

The three-act structure helps to give the story a clear beginning, middle, and end and helps to keep the plot moving forward.

Additionally, the three-act structure helps to build tension and create a satisfying resolution for the reader. Without a clear structure, a story can feel disjointed or confusing, so the three act structure helps to keep the story organised and focused.

Ten chapters within these three acts allow for correct and accurate character arcs and the creation of plot "beats."

There is no obligation for you to stick to this prescriptive way of planning your content. These guidelines will help you to plan the major plot points. The outline planner is flexible enough for you to add chapters on either side of the numbered chapters in this workbook. If you wanted your book to be twenty or thirty chapters, you can make it so. You should do so within the correct act so that your novel contains all the right "beats" in all the right places.

Please feel free to tweak the outline planner in any way you feel will help you the most. Add in your personal touches where it feels right.

After you have completed the outline planner, you can get cracking on writing your story. Writer's block should be a thing of the past when you have a clear line of sight through your novel. Most of all, your editor will be able to see your intentions. This will put them in a much better position to see how to best assist you in your developmental edit.

So, let's waste no more time and dive right into act 1, which covers chapters 1 to 3.

Act 1
CHAPTERS 1-3

The main aim of act 1 in a novel is to introduce the main characters and set the stage for the rest of the story. This includes establishing the setting, introducing key characters and their relationships, and establishing the main conflict or problem that the story will focus on.

Act 1 is also known as the "setup" or "exposition" of the story and is designed to establish the foundations for the rest of the story to build upon. It helps to introduce the reader to the world and characters of the story and gives them a sense of what to expect as the story progresses.

Start this act by considering who your main character is. What does their everyday look like? We call it their boring, average day. Think about what their baseline is.

For the duration of 'Part Two - The Complete Plan' we will be using the term 'antagonist' and 'villain' throughout to indicate the same character.

Chapter 1

You want your opening line to contain active, exciting words. Dialogue works well. Aim to capture the reader's attention immediately. This is a good time to put yourself in the reader's position.

What type of line would capture your attention from the get-go? Also, consider who else will be in the opening scene. This could give you ideas of how to write that opening line. Is it going to be a question asked by one character to the other? A statement? A warning? Or a threat, even?

Introduce the setting, weather and location after this line. Start to world-build for the reader.

World-building is the process of creating the fictional world in which a story takes place. This includes developing the setting, culture, history, laws, customs, and geography of the world, as well as the characters and their relationships within it. World-building is an important aspect of storytelling because it helps to create a believable and immersive world for the reader to engage with. It helps to make the story feel more realistic and adds depth and complexity to the characters and their actions.

Describe the noises around the characters in this opening scene. If there aren't any sounds then explain this lack of atmosphere. A good tip from us here when you are writing your opening scene is to free-write at this point. You are flexing your writing muscles, getting the feel for the keys on your computer, or the pen in your hand. You are playing about with ideas and getting the tone right. At this point, there is no room for definitive word choices or pretty writing. Write ugly here. Make tonnes of spelling mistakes, to the point where underlined in red, is every other word on your screen. Or your handwritten notes look like a scrawl. We can hone and craft our opening at a later stage, but for now, let's concentrate on getting the words flowing out of us. **Don't edit, just write.**

Next, we can expand on the description of the main character. By now, if you've followed the steps in the workbook, you will have a clear idea of who your main character is.

You will know what they look like, and the positive/negative traits that make them who they are. Think about what accent they have, their height/weight/build, and what clothes they like to wear. Be as descriptive as possible at this point. This is the first "meeting" your readers have with the main protagonist. They will need to picture them and imagine them as 3D people to invest in them while they battle the "enemy."

Make your main character as relatable as possible using the powers of description. What are your main character's internal and external goals? Look back to your planning notes in part 1 of your workbook to help with this section. It's the reason why you completed it.

Now, the 'wallop scene.' This is a phrase we coined ourselves to explain the thunderbolt scene that sets the reader up for the ride of their life. The epic car crash, explosion or bombshell (literal or metaphorical).

You want them to sit back and go "wow! I never saw that coming!" You've set up the baseline for the main character in the first few paragraphs of the first chapter, what their normal, average day looks like. Now let's throw in a wallop moment. Something that would completely disrupt their life and all those around them. **Don't be shy, make it a whopper!**

In **'Goddess Of The Moon,'** our wallop scene involves our main character, Aria, finding out she is a member of a sinister cult, one that is destroying everything in their path. Not what the reader would expect from the hero, to be involved in a bad deed, and certain to shock them (the reader) into paying attention. We will then skip forward to Aria working out a way to rebel against this evil cult.

Once we have invested the reader in the story events so far, we can introduce the antagonist. What is their height, weight, and build? What accent do they have, and what clothes do they wear? What is the reason they've decided to act against the main character? What are the other characters' reactions to your antagonist?

In **'Goddess Of The Moon,'** our antagonist is Rohan, the evil cult's leader. His aim in the story is to achieve ultimate power over the empire. We will describe him as ruthless and patient at first, as the takeover of the empire is met with little resistance as the people of the forest are compliant at first, but as Aria's powers grow, and the resistance becomes more forceful against him, Rohan becomes as unpleasant, impatient and indiscriminately murderous. This evolution of Rohan's character helps to set up his arc, as over time he realises the resistance is gaining momentum, threatening his ambitions of total dominance.

At this point in the chapter, we want to set up our first plot twist. This is so that when it occurs in the narrative it will be believable for the reader. Write in the workbook here what would need to happen for the plot twist you are planning for later to work. You want to take your readers on a journey through your story and keep them engaged and invested. If you don't set up your plot twist then it won't have the desired effect on the reader.

We are at the point in the story where we need an 'inciting event' to occur.

What is an inciting event?

An inciting event is a significant event or moment in a story that sets the plot in motion and triggers the main conflict or problem. It is typically the first major event in the story and is often referred to as the "catalyst" or "point of no return." The inciting event is what initiates the action of the story and helps to establish the main characters and their motivations. It is typically a turning point in the story that drives the characters towards their goals and sets the stage for the rest of the story to unfold.

Examples of inciting events:

- A character discovers a mysterious object that sets them on a quest to uncover the truth
- A character receives a letter or message that reveals a shocking secret
- A character witnesses a crime or injustice and decides to take action
- A character is faced with a difficult decision that changes the course of their life
- A character experiences a personal loss or trauma that drives them towards a new goal
- A character receives an unexpected opportunity or challenge that pushes them out of their comfort zone
- A character is faced with a life-threatening situation that forces them to take action
- A character meets a new person who introduces them to a new way of thinking or living

Ask yourself the following questions:

- What lessons does your main character need to learn and why?
- What are the consequences if they don't figure out the problem?
- Who else is in the scene?
- What is the stake?
- Is there a stake in the proceedings?

Use the five senses to set the scene here. In **'Goddess Of The Moon'** our inciting event is the discovery by Aria that the cult is wiping out any resistance to them whilst they carry out their takeover. Her horror in finding this out, and her determination to do something about it, ignites the narrative spark and sets up her external goal of stopping Rohan's evil plan.

In our sensory detail, we can describe the noises made by Aria when she finds out the cult is slowly eradicating her friends and family in the forest. We can include any gasps, crying, surprise, or shrieks of anger when she finds out about the pain and suffering her people are going through.

With your narrative, write in who is present in your scene, what are they wearing, and how are they acting.

Our inciting event leads the reader to think, 'what's going to happen now?' Will Aria react in anger and put more of her people, the ones who follow her, in danger? Or, will this inciting event be the making of her? How is the discovery of this sinister cult going to affect the rest of the characters in the story? The inciting event will dictate what direction the story is going to travel in.

Start to introduce secondary characters as you plan the fallout of your inciting event. For **'Goddess Of The Moon,'** we will introduce more characters in the story as Aria begins to plan the fight back. These extra characters will include helpers or even allies to the antagonist.

In your novel plan, consider how your extra characters will help proceedings and what they add to the narrative. Sprinkle in contrasting character traits to spice up your narrative. What internal and external goals do these new characters have?

You can include an impact scene here, now you have your new characters added to your story.

An impact scene is the scene that happens immediately after an important scene. It can tell a reader a lot about a character.

For example, if a supposedly 'confident' character has done a speech on stage in front of hundreds of people that would be 'the scene', but the impact scene would be immediately after them coming off stage and having a panic attack, showing a deeper part of their character and letting the reader in to the characters vulnerable side.

The impact scene in **'Goddess Of The Moon'** is in the forest when Aria makes a promise to the elder gods that she will stop at nothing to defeat Rohan and bring peace back to the people of the forest. Her eyes are red with tears of anger and frustration, her fists clenched with determination.

Here, you want to go hard at the visceral descriptions of your character's reactions to the main event of your wallop scene. What are the characters' wants and needs now? How will they go forward? What conversations are happening? Include also what your antagonist is doing at this point. Ensure you are subtle, as you don't want the reader to figure out their ulterior motives too soon. Include here what's at stake.

Let's return to your plot twist idea, the one you set up earlier. Throw it in here. Shake up the action.

Chapter 2

Think about what your **motivation** is for writing this scene. What purpose does it serve in the plot and narrative of your story? How will this scene move the story on? You should start to world-build here a bit for your antagonist. This gives variety to the reader. They go from chapter one learning about the main character and the main conflict, to now learning who is also involved. They also learn how the world of the antagonist works. This offers contrasts in the narrative and helps to build the character arcs. As you build this world, remember that everything has to exist in the storyline for a reason.

Chapter two should include how your main character slowly changes as relationships begin to develop. New personalities and back stories start to emerge and we start to see who *really* gets on with who, and where the enemies in the forest lie. Plan in here what your main character will do about these factors. Who will they align with? Why?

Here is a good time to drop in a few references to the main character's key traits. If you have a character who used to run every morning but their relationship/life/friends/job have been wearing them down, so they don't do it as much now, mention this and why to reflect this change. You could show rather than tell this by writing in a scene where the character's running buddy leaves them a voicemail asking where they are. Have your main character roll over in bed ignoring the incoming message. It might not seem like a big, important scene, but it shows how the circumstances in the story are affecting your main character's personality.

Changes in behaviour will address your main character's key inner conflicts and develop/evolve them. That conflict can also manifest itself as outer conflict as the story wears on. Plan here for there to be a major development with the case. This can be where the main character might have to go outside their comfort zone to get the result they need. This external goal may need them to interact with other characters, good or bad. Who are they and what role will they play here? Use this space in your workbook to reflect on how this goal is affecting other characters. Describe how the daily life of all involved is changing now.

How do you plan for these plot developments to affect the villain at this point in the story? Write in your workbook all your ideas here.

In our example novel, **'Goddess Of The Moon'** our villain, Rohan, may seem quite interested in an alliance with Aria, to keep her onside. He might even offer her an elevated position at his side, to keep her compliant.

Your main character's 'fatal flaw' will crop up at this point. Your planning should reflect how they plan to overcome this flaw to ensure they can continue with their day-to-day. If your main character's fatal flaw is that they are too quick to jump to conclusions when they see two people discussing a secret then misunderstandings will set the cat amongst the pigeons and therefore cause conflict, keeping you readers invested in the story.

As we reach the end of chapter two we want to set up a cliffhanger to keep the readers hooked so they read on. Throw in a revelation that will keep the reader engaged. Think of it like when an episode of your favourite drama series ends.

What events will make you continue to watch the next episode?

Chapter 3

The third chapter in act one includes the same starting point as the others:

- Opening line and scene
- Which characters appear
- What your motivation is for writing this scene

Including these key elements will ensure you are setting out your intentions and staying in control of your plot. This will cut out any possibility of a huge plot hole appearing in the middle, or worse, at the end of your story.

Everything you write must have a purpose.

This purpose is to drive the narrative forward. You want to propel the reader through the events and towards the resolution. You are in the driving seat but they have paid for a riveting ride don't forget. So it's your responsibility to provide this, without any annoying detours into a plot hole.

You could liken plot holes even to potholes in the road. When you hit a pothole it jars you and feels uncomfortable. If you hit it at speed it will cause damage to your car which is frustrating and leads you to swear and grumble. For readers, this experience is quite similar when they hit a plot hole in the story. It makes them second-guess themselves, and read back over the book to check it's *you* that's got it wrong, not them. It is very frustrating for a reader and there isn't any excuse for it if you, as the author, have done your due diligence. You can't blame your editor, even if you think they have missed it too. Correct, adequate and careful planning by following the steps in your workbook will stop plot holes from appearing in your writing.

In chapter three we will **discover a new goal** for the main character, and how this new goal affects the others in the story. Are they opposed to it? Are any accusations, or arguments, at this point? Does the main character face any consequences if the new goal isn't achieved? Again, use the space in your workbook to thrash out your ideas here.

Write in what happens if this new goal fails. We want to keep the conflict present in every scene we write. Fantasy fiction stories have to be resolved in order to get to the satisfying ending that readers hope for. Problems have to be faced and overcome, and villains need to be defeated for the world order to be restored. You want it to be where there's conflict and there are some ideas that are being thrown around that not everybody agrees with. And this is what can make a plot interesting. It's not going to be seamless and effortless. There are going to be some disagreements.

Don't forget to include what your villain is doing at this point when you introduce this new goal for the main character. How do they react? Does it throw them off? Do they start to crack? How are they changing the events as the story is progressing? What are they feeling, doing and saying? Is the villain throwing in some suggestions that seem to be encouraging peace and compliance, but underneath we actually know that they're planning world domination?

The new goal in **'Goddess Of The Moon'** could be Aria's mission to save the healer, Fae, from the evil cult's clutches.

We can put this new desire in the next space in the workbook, which addresses the 'slight hope' that occurs in chapter three. This is the breakthrough moment the main character needed to "progress the mission".

In **'Goddess Of The Moon**,' Aria discovers that the further away from the cult she is, the stronger her powers become. Her new understanding of her power helps to progress the narrative into the next phase of her character arc.

Now the chapter must end on a cliffhanger, again to keep the reader engrossed in the plot.

In **'Goddess Of The Moon'** we could write a scene where the antagonist, Rohan, realises Aria has escaped the forest and sends his army of followers after her. Rohan has raised the stakes and orders the following army to kill Aria on sight, switching the narrative up a gear and adding extra peril to Aria's quest to overthrow Rohan and his evil cult.

Think about what your cliffhanger is going to be. Make it a good one!

Act 2
CHAPTERS 4-6

In a novel, the main aim of Act 2 is to further the plot and build conflict. This is typically accomplished by introducing new characters or plot twists, or by deepening the conflict between the main characters.

Act 2 is often considered the "meat" of the story, as it is where the main conflicts and challenges are faced by the characters. It is also where the main character begins to take action to resolve the conflicts and move the story forward. In general, the main aim of Act 2 is to keep the reader engaged and invested in the story, and to build tension and suspense as the story progresses.

Act two centres itself on what's known as the 'emotional journey' of the main character. In this act, you must give your characters all sorts of challenges to overcome.

In short, this is the act where the mood changes. Act one sets everything up. characters are introduced, scenes set and the main question is posed. Act two is where everything changes with the things you have established in act one.

Chapter 4

As in the previous chapters, start chapter four by planning:

- The opening line/scene
- Setting out what characters appear
- What your motivation is for writing this chapter

We are almost at the midpoint of our three-act, ten-chapter novel plan here, so now we need to set off some fireworks.

The plan to set up the main character and the villain on a collision course, potentially involving a near-miss. The wheels have come off the "mission" in a big way. What has caused this? And is it because of the main character's Achilles heel? Has their fatal flaw become a game-changer? Which other characters get caught up in the crossfire?

For our example novel, **'Goddess Of The Moon,'** we could use Aria's fatal flaw (her being impulsive when it comes to approaching the enemy) as the reason why she is almost captured by Rohan's army. Aria's almost-capture means she and Caden are in placed in mortal danger and the mission is close to failure.

In your novel plan, who now will be to blame for the mission going wrong? How and why? What did they do or not do?

At this point in the story, we can have:

- massive arguments
- epic fallouts within alliances
- tempers flaring all around the land

We want to turn the conflict dial up to maximum here. Who forgot to do what? What were the consequences? Who left a trail through the forest leading Rohan's army to where Caden and Aria are sheltering? Who has messed up here?

How close were your characters to success? How could you show this in your plot and narrative? What is your main character doing in this chapter? How are they involved in the plan going wrong? Are they at fault? How do they rectify the situation?

Time to think about what your antagonist is doing in this chapter. What are they thinking, saying, or doing now? Sprinkle in some odd conversations between the villain and the people around them where they could look like they're helping. Have them making a magic potion, or healing a wounded member of their army. Make the reader think that this character is multi-faceted. They are trying to help, even though their intentions are predominantly evil. Even bad guys aren't completely evil. There are some grey areas in their personality and actions. This is what makes them so interesting.

Time for plot twist two. **You need to make it a big one.** A completely unexpected one. Make your plot twist completely unpredictable.

What would be the **worst thing** that could happen right now? What would derail the main character's progress, plan, or strategy? Time to write any emotions your main character's feeling right now. After the plot twist, what happened? Why? Who is at fault?

To choose an idea for your plot twist, circle back to your character's internal and external motivations planning page in your workbook. Here you will have ideas for "what's the worst thing that could happen here." Choose one of these and stick it in here.

Time to seal off the chapter with an epic ending. It all seems too much for the main character and their allies to face finding a solution to the plot twist. What does the main character say and do here? What are the reactions, and responses from the allies? Make your main character do something out of character due to the stress of the situation.

Make their flaw comes to the forefront.

Chapter 5

In this chapter, we must think of a new goal that your main character has arrived at. Have they had some thinking time? Did they go back to the village where it all began and it was by the river they'd grown up swimming in that they figured it all out? The villain's evil plan has been found out before they can deploy it and they have dropped themselves right in it. What conversations are taking place between the main character and their primary ally?

In **'Goddess Of The Moon,'** this is Caden, Aria's best friend powerful ally, and the voice of reason.

Think about why your primary ally is helping your main character. What conversations are taking place? From your internal and external goals planning for your sidekick, you'll have ideas. Does your primary ally feel guilty about something in their past? They want to pay something forward, and they want to try and help their friend defeat their sworn enemy? Circle back to your notes to help you with this.

After all, that's why we've created part one in the workbook; to help you with part two.

Think about what the **resistance is to the new goal.** How will this test your main character and why? We will now throw in a red herring.

Red herrings are narrative techniques/plot devices that send your readers down the wrong path to figuring out who is scuppering the happy ending. We use them to deflect what is going on. The key to good red herring use is to not over-use it. Throw in one or two, at different points in the story. By doing this you will set up an excellent adventure for your readers to enjoy, from all the breadcrumbs you drop for them. You want to make the reader start to question somebody's motives in the story.

Moving on now to the 'new goal' for the main character, based on the back of the inclusion of a red herring. What does this new goal look like on a day-to-day basis? Who is involved? What is your antagonist doing during this time? Are they behaving? Your main character may get a couple of small wins during the pursuit of this new goal. What are these wins? The new plan seems to be a good idea. What is the resistance to the new goal? How will this test your main character and why?

To help you with filling in ideas in this section, head on back to the section in the workbook that deals with positive and negative traits.

What is testing your characters at this point? How can you show this? Don't say that they struggle with this; *show that they are struggling.* Make your writing active. Make your reader part of them struggling.

'Show not tell' examples to help you:

- **Happiness:** "A wide grin spread across Mary's face as she skipped down the street, her laughter ringing out like bells on a sunny day."
- **Sadness:** "Tears streamed down John's face as he clutched the letter in his hand, his shoulders shaking with silent sobs."
- **Anger:** "Sarah's fists clenched at her sides as she glared at the offending object, her breath coming in short, angry gasps."
- **Fear:** "Mike's heart pounded in his chest as he backed away from the growling dog, his legs trembling beneath him."

- **Love:** "As Jane looked into Tom's eyes, she felt a warmth spread through her chest, a feeling of love and belonging overwhelming her."
- **Joy:** "As the confetti rained down and the crowd cheered, Emma threw her head back and let out a joyful whoop, her face radiant with happiness."
- **Nostalgia:** "As he leafed through the old photo album, Jack couldn't help but smile at the memories that flooded back. He could almost smell the freshly baked cookies and feel the warmth of the summer sun on his skin."
- **Envy:** "Green with envy, Rachel couldn't help but glare at her friend's new car, her lips pressed into a tight, bitter line."
- **Disgust**: "The smell of rotten eggs filled the air as Jane wrinkled her nose in disgust, her stomach churning at the sight of the mouldy food."
- **Frustration:** "As the computer froze for the third time that day, Jake let out an angry sigh and slammed his fist on the desk, his frustration mounting."

We are at the end of chapter five now and the villain does something super nasty. How and why? Who is involved? What conversations are happening? What is the impact of this attack? Think of your end line and **make it a whopper.**

The 'attack' from the villain could be:

Literal: they could hurt the main character so their loyal band of followers won't trust them anymore.

Metaphorical: they go on a charm offensive to try and convince the main character, or their followers, into joining their alliance instead.

Either way, the antagonist is getting worried now. The net is closing and they need to think fast. The worry and panic of being overthrown may lead your villain to make some unwise decisions. Think about what they could be, and what the outcome of those decisions is.

Chapter 6

We now conclude act two. Time to plan what the impact of the villain's attack on the main character is. Was it a physical attack? Or some other approach, such as embarrassing them. Let your creative mind go wild here. Who else does the attack affect? The ally? Other minor characters? Are they collateral damage in the villain's pursuit of dominance? What does life look like now for your other characters?

This last part of act two is the time to show how events have changed the characters in your story. They would have started a certain way in act one. Now lies, betrayal and potential broken loyalties have altered them forever. Has anyone died or lost someone they loved? Has the antagonist struck again, taking away another loved one from their family/tribe? Think of the fallout from this on the characters left behind.

What is the main point of difference in your main character since the first act? Are they battle-hardened now? Are they wiser? Are they more experienced? Are they more informed on the villain's plots or flaws? This is where, if you know how your character acts in act one, you write how are they changing exactly. For example, if they're a bit of a clean freak in act one, are they starting to let themselves go now at the end of act two? Are they starting to lose their cool a lot more frequently with their allies now? You want to show that something is affecting them at this stage of the novel.

Come back to the villain now. What are they saying or doing? How is their behaviour different from how it was in act one, chapter one, and why is this? What does your main character need to do now? Time to up the stakes. Spell out the consequences if they don't act. What happens if their plan goes wrong? You want to make the reader buy into the consequences. Could it be somebody else has been betrayed or killed? Whatever it is, make it huge.

You are now going to plan your ending to act two. It has to be a massive wallop. Make your readers think. **Make them question everything they already know.**

Act 3
CHAPTERS 7-10

In a novel, the main aim of Act 3 is to resolve the conflicts and plot points introduced in earlier acts and bring the story to a satisfying conclusion. This is typically accomplished by having the main character take further action to resolve the conflicts, and by bringing together all of the various threads of the plot.

Act 3 is often considered the "climax" of the story, as it is where the main character faces their greatest challenges and the stakes are at their highest. In general, the main aim of Act 3 is to bring the story to a satisfying conclusion, and to wrap up any remaining loose ends or plot points.

Here, your characters will face their 'final epic battle' with the enemy. They will overcome the threat that has formed the basis of your novel.

Chapter 7

A hive of activity will happen here in the big countdown to the finale. Note down what the specifics are and what happens if the clock ticks down to zero. Time to explain what the master plan to defeat the villain is. Include conversations with naysayers, those characters who doubt the success of the plan. What arguments are taking place?

Move on now to what would happen if this plan **fails**. You want to make it where it is a huge consequence. If you think of action movies, if the plan fails it's the end of the world. That's a pretty big consequence. That investment is what you want the readers to feel.

What is the villain thinking and doing at this final stage? Even if they're not in the scene, detail what the villain will be thinking now the plan is at risk of being foiled.

Next, we can allow our main character to achieve a victory in the story. Something that has finally gone the right way for the main character. This is the thing that has been troubling the ally throughout about the main character. Has their trust been rewarded or betrayed?

In **'Goddess Of The Moon,'** everyone in the resistance tribe is giving advice to Aria. Which advice is she listening to?

Time to describe your story's version of this scene in detail. For example, who is present etc…. You can use this scene a bit later as a contrast to when, for example, the ally finds out something devastating. This can be the key element of the third massive plot twist. This is where happy, celebratory feelings will change to despair, as the story propels itself towards the final denouement.

Make plot twist three huge. What could happen now that would blow the "victory" out of the water?

Has the main character trusted someone in their tribe who has turned out to be a traitor? Has someone else come forward and revealed their betrayal? What could be the worst repercussion possible?

Make it as unpredictable as possible. Plan in here this plot twist affects and why? How does it impact the main character's external goal? What conversations are happening between the main character and the main ally?

As long as your massive plot twist makes sense in the story world then anything goes here. Remember your responsibility to the reader. They will always appreciate a clever, foreshadowed, plot twist. Or a plot twist that takes their breath away. It can be as unpredictable as you like. What the reader won't accept is a plot twist that goes against everything they believe to be true so far. It would jar with their understanding of the characters and plot. Head scratchers are good, but eye-squinting, 'meh" twists not so much.

You want to keep your readers on their toes with the lead-up to the twist. Then make their jaw hit the floor when the big reveal happens.

Now to plan what conversations are taking place after this plot twist. With whom are these conversations taking place, and why? What is the main character's external goal now? How has it changed from the revelation of the plot twist and what does your main character have to do now? There has been another sting in the tail for the main character and the ally's quest. The situation starts to go from bad to worse for the main character. Now they have to readjust to this new predicament. Plan in here what this might include. Morale could drop and arguments could start to happen. Friends start to fall out with each other perhaps?

Chapter 8

This is where the story starts to ramp up in urgency, as we are drawing nearer to the final battle. What conversations are taking place between your characters now the stakes have been raised?

The clock is ticking down and the race is on to stop the villain winning the day. To ramp up the pressure more, plan how the situation goes from bad to worse for the main character. Does the villain strike? To add an extra dynamic, you could bring someone back from act one of your story, so that their presence in the story makes more sense. Someone who didn't like or trust your main character's motives or ability to win the battle, and now they have come good. What almost happens? Add in an occurrence of crossed wires for two of your characters here to keep the readers on the edge of their seats.

Finally, we are at the point in the story where your main character and the villain meet face-to-face in the final battle. How will this play out?

In our example, **'Goddess Of The Moon,'** this could be where Rohan finally catches up with Aria and Caden. **This is the scene that the reader has been waiting for**.

For this reason, your end line must hit hard. What could this line involve? Try and avoid the cliched, "It wasn't you, it was me!" type of line. Or even the, "I knew it was going to be you who was behind all this." This will turn your reader right off. Don't lose them now with a weak line.

Chapter 9

This chapter moves us closer to the conclusion of our fantasy fiction novel. But we're not done yet with the twists and turns for your main character. It is about to go wrong for them in this final battle. What's worse is it is their own fault. Did they forget to take their enchanted sword into battle? Did they accidentally leave the armour they were going to need in the forest? This is where you can bring back into proceedings your main character's "fatal flaw."

Elaborate here on that flaw and how it has become their undoing. Is anyone else affected by this? Did anyone get caught in the drama?

In our example, **'Goddess Of The Moon,'** this is where Aria's impulsivity leads to Caden's death.

Revisit your planning pages on internal/external goals here, and note down if any have been achieved. Which positive and negative traits are on show here, and are they part of the reason for the undoing?

What inner demons and/or conflicts does your main character have to wrestle with once and for all to defeat the antagonist?

What are the other characters doing right now? What would the villain be feeling? Would they be feeling smug? Would they be feeling threatened? Would they be feeling on the defensive? Your main character will have to fix things now, using all their resources. How will they do this? What has to happen? Did it go right? The clock is ticking again now. Time to ramp up the pressure. What is going on in the background? Which characters are affected by the ticking clock? Write in the arguments that the characters are having about a possible new but crazy-sounding plan to stop the antagonist once and for all.

Chapter 10

So here we are, we arrive at the tenth and final chapter. This a good time to remind you that it's fine to have more chapters threaded between these ten major chapters. As we stated at the beginning of our outline planner, there is no exact science to this. But writing within a three-act structure will ensure your novel is well-paced and hits all the right beats at the right stages. Ten chapters is a ballpark figure, based on the research we have carried out. But if you want to experiment with shorter chapters, meaning there are more in number in your novel, then go for it. Ensure though, that they include the same elements as these in the workbook.

This will make sure your novel maintains its momentum from start to finish.

Let's think now about how to end your novel. Your main character needs to defeat the villain once and for all so it's time to gather the troops. Send out a rallying cry to all available friends and allies from all surrounding lands to thwart the antagonist.

How does the main character rally their allies? What is said during the heartfelt speech? Do the other characters get swayed by the speech? Don't forget to refer to the ticking clock. Time is running out. What is the villain doing during this speech? Even if they don't appear in the scene, you want to be knowing how would they be reacting. Would they be pacing up and down? Would they be planning something?

The next part is the carrying out of the plan. What happens? How close do the characters come to time running out?

Now it's time to throw in **one last plot twist** when everything is about to be resolved. **Make it humungous.** What if, when needed, the "thing" wasn't there? Or the magic spell that has been relied upon to bring the dark times to an end actually doesn't work?

Are you brave enough to bump off a key, beloved character like we have in our workbook example? Go on, kill your darlings!

One last push. The clock is almost at zero. One or two of your characters are about to become unlikely heroes. Who are they? How do they assist the main character?

This is it now, the antagonist's last stand. The duel is almost over for them. Defeat is on the cards. But, it's never that simple, right? What last surprises are there? Are any cats pulled out of the bag for the villain to win the day? What is the villain thinking, feeling, or saying right now?

Use as much sensory detail as you can here. What is going on? What are they feeling? What are they hearing?

Victory! The day is won. How does this final battle with the antagonist pan out? Who dies? Who survives? Write out how the main character shows how they would've changed since the first act. Write in your last line. Will you leave the action on the cliffhanger? If you are planning to write a fantasy fiction series then this is a good place to set up the next book. If you are writing a standalone then do not leave it on a cliffhanger, as what would be the point? You might think it is clever writing but it will frustrate your reader. They have come this far with you and at some point, the roller-coaster needs to come back into the dock. Let them off with good memories of your writing, so that they feel compelled to buy your next book.

Your complete novel outline is now planned. You have enough meat on the skeleton now to begin writing. The next part of this guide will help you to decide how long your novel should be, so again you are fitting in with the conventions of the fantasy fiction genre.

Word Count

Having the correct word count for your genre is crucial to understand. Pacing-wise, your book will hit all the right notes within the standard length of a book in your genre. It also means the books will look similar in thickness. It will look strange on a bookshelf if one book is 65,000 words and the next book in the series is 125,000. Better off splitting the second book into two and having a three-part series.

Fantasy fiction novels tend to include lots of world-building, and lengthy descriptions of mythical lands and beasts.

So, from our research into the fantasy fiction genre, we have found that the word count sweet spot is **90,000 - 100,000 words.** Again, this is a rough guide and you won't lose any fans if you push that to 110,000 or 120,000. The point here is it isn't over 150,000 as you will need to sharpen up your narrative if this is happening, unless you are writing an epic fantasy.

If you were to create a writing schedule for completing your novel, it works out to between 22,500 and 25,000 words written per week.

You will complete your book in four weeks if you write five times a week and you write between 4,500 and 5,000 words each session.

Simple, right? So what are you waiting for?

PART III

After You Have Written Your Novel

How To Write A Synopsis

After you've written your novel, you're going to need a synopsis.

A lot of writers find this quite difficult to do, but it is crucial to get right. It can make a literary agent accept you onto their register if you want to go traditionally published. Or if you decide to enter your novel in a competition and want to make a good impression, you will need a synopsis for them to judge.

A synopsis is an overview of your entire novel's plotline. It should include:

- The main characters
- The main events
- The key turning points
- Plot twists that occur in the story

It should include a comprehensive overview of the ending too. This will include all 'spoilers' and plot twist reveals.

A synopsis is not a blurb. A blurb, as we will see when we go into more detail later, is a cleverly crafted piece of description that goes on your novel's back cover. A blurb is designed to entice the reader to buy your book because they're dying to know what will happen.

A blurb doesn't give away the ending, whereas a synopsis will. They're designed for different audiences.

Your synopsis should include:

- Meaningful and interesting characters
- A clear arc to the story
- A satisfying conclusion or a decent cliffhanger if you intend your book to be part of a series.

When would you need to write a synopsis?

If you wanted to send your book idea to a publishing company or enter your novel into a competition, the standard rule is to send in the first three chapters and a one-to-two-page synopsis. This is so a judge or a publishing agent can read the start of your book and get a feel for your writing and the level of your marketable talent.

A synopsis intends to give an overview of the plot, characters, arcs and outcomes of the whole novel. It is a crucial tool for the agent or judge to gauge if your novel is worthy of a publishing deal. It is also used to help a judge determine if your work should go forward to the next phase of the competition, where the judges will spend time reading the whole of your novel.

The synopsis is vital to get right so it shows your novel in the best light possible to people in the industry. Remember, they have limited time to spend on the thousands of manuscripts they get sent every day. **You must make your novel stand out by writing a strong and effective synopsis.**

So, how do you write a strong synopsis?

Paragraph 1 needs to introduce your two main characters; your hero and villain. You need to give details on what event has happened that will start your story – this is your 'wallop scene'.

Outline what the location of this event is and where the main characters start from. When is all this happening? What are the characters doing, and thinking when they hear of or are caught up in this wallop scene?

> **PARAGRAPH 1**
> - Introduce your two main characters - hero and villain.
> - What event has happened that will start your story? Wallop scene?
> - What is the location of this event, or where do the main characters start from?
> - When is all of this happening?
> - What are the characters doing/thinking when they hear of/are caught up in this wallop scene?

Paragraph 2 of your synopsis needs to detail your main character's plan to tackle the event. Write in also what your main villain is planning to do as a response. How are they both going to go about it? Here, include your main plot points. Where, when and why are they going to follow this action plan? What other characters are involved in this action plan?

> **PARAGRAPH 2**
> - What is your main character's plan to tackle the event?
> - What is your main villain planning to do in response?
> - How are they both going to go about it? Here include your main plot points.
> - Where/when/why are they going to follow this action plan?
> - What other characters are involved in this action plan?

In **Paragraph 3** of your synopsis, you must outline how the story will end. How does the hero win the day? It's now time to circle back to the wallop scene from paragraph 1. How have things changed? What happens to the villain? Is there a cliffhanger ending?

> **PARAGRAPH 3**
>
> - How will the story end? How does the hero win the day?
> - Now time to circle back to the wallop scene - how have things changed?
> - What happens to the villain? Is there to be a cliffhanger ending?
> - Do not leave the ending of your novel as a mystery - the agent or judge will want to know how your story will end.
> - Include all the spoilers, cliffhangers and plot twist reveals - you want the agent/judge to enjoy your premise.

Under no circumstances must you leave the ending of your synopsis a mystery. The agent or judge will want to know how your story will end. Include all the spoilers, cliffhangers and plot twist reveals. You want the agent or judge to enjoy your premise and be able to see your vision. They are not reading your synopsis for pleasure. They are cold, analytical and judgemental as professionals, so give them everything. If you don't, they will have no way of judging what would have happened in your book and whether it was an award-winner if you keep the best bits secret.

In your workbook, you have a 'your turn' page to write out your full synopsis.

For the purposes of this guide, we have written a synopsis of **'Goddess Of The Moon,'** to give you an idea of how it is done.

GODDESS OF THE MOON: LUNA'S GUIDE TO ARIA'S ESCAPE
A FANTASY ADVENTURE NOVEL FOR YOUNG ADULTS

Aria is a member of a cult in the forest, led by the ruthless Rohan. When she discovers that she is the only one with the magic necessary to overthrow the leaders, she embarks on an epic journey to save Fae, a healer targeted by the cult's dark spirits.

Along the way, Aria meets Caden, who becomes a powerful ally in her quest. As they learn about the cult's dark history and form a powerful alliance, they face death threats and challenges on their journey to escape.

With the guidance of the goddess Luna, Aria and Caden defeat Rohan and his followers, but their victory is short-lived as they soon discover a larger conflict brewing with the cult's shadowy leader, the Emperor.

As they prepare for war, Aria and Caden are trained by powerful sorcerers in the ancient magic of the mystical mountain. But as they delve deeper into the mountain's secrets, they uncover a shocking truth about the Emperor and his true power.

In a final showdown, Aria and Caden use the ancient magic of the moon to defeat the Emperor and his minions, but not before Caden is killed by the traitorous Fae.

Aria is left to carry on their mission alone, determined to honour Caden's sacrifice and protect those in need.

We will now talk about how to write a blurb. This is what you can put on the back cover of your book to give the reader a snapshot of your book. The intention is to entice them enough to give you a shot and buy it.

How To Write A Blurb

A blurb is a cleverly crafted piece of description that goes on your novel's back cover. It is short, fitting snugly on the back of your book, and is designed to work as a promotional tool to entice your reader to buy your book. If, after they've read your book's blurb, your reader cannot bear to leave your book on the shelf because they need to know what will happen, then you have written a successful blurb.

A blurb will use:

- Attention-grabbing power words
- Will often use question marks and exclamation marks
- Will often use an ellipsis to leave a reader asking questions

You need to send a final copy of your blurb so your cover designer can place it on the back of your book. You can also use your blurb as part of your book description on the selling platform of your choice. You may even use your blurb to advertise your book in a newsletter and/or on your website or blog site.

In your workbook, you will see that we have included some example blurbs. We have broken them down into their parts, so you can see where each goes.

So, how do you write a strong blurb?

In the **first line or paragraph** of your blurb, you should introduce your hero, and describe what their professional role is. Next, drop in some adjectives to describe their appearance and personality. Include here what makes them so interesting or what sets them apart from the rest. Are they unlikely heroes?

> **IN THE FIRST LINE/PARAGRAPH**
> - Introduce your hero.
> - Describe what his profession or role is.
> - Next, drop in some adjectives to describe his appearance and his personality. Include here what makes him so interesting or what sets him apart from the rest. Is he an unlikely hero perhaps?

In the **second line or paragraph**, reveal the setting of your novel. Introduce the period and the main location of the action. You may want to world-build for the reader at this point.

Next, reveal the current situation with the hero and what their life is like. What dreams, aspirations or desires do they have? Are those dreams about to be destroyed? If so, how? Remember your power words. Ramp up the threat level as you go through your setup.

> **IN THE SECOND LINE/PARAGRAPH**
> - **Reveal the setting. Introduce the time period and the main location of the action. If you are writing fantasy or science fiction you may want to world-build for the reader.**
> - **Next, reveal the current situation with the hero, i.e. what's his life like?**
> - **What dreams, aspirations or desires does he have? Are they about to be destroyed? If so, how? Remember your power words.**
> - **Ramp up the threat level as you go through your set-up.**

In the third line or paragraph, define what turns the situation on its head. What turns the hero's life inside out? What external goal are they trying to achieve? How does this impact their internal goal? What is standing in the way of them achieving these goals?

> **IN THE THIRD LINE/PARAGRAPH**
> - **Define what turns the situation on its head - what turns the hero's life inside out?**
> - **What external goal is he trying to achieve?**
> - **How does this impact on his internal goal?**
> - **What is standing in the way of him achieving these goals?**

In the last line or paragraph, what is at stake? Aim to hit home with this, using the power words and questions that you want the reader to ask.

> **IN THE LAST LINE/PARAGRAPH**
> - **What is at stake? Really hit home with this using power words and questions that you want the reader to ask.**

To help you further, we have written a blurb for our example book, **'Goddess Of The Moon.'**

The first paragraph of our blurb is as follows:

> **When Aria discovers that she is a member of a sinister cult deep in the forest, she knows she must escape before it's too late. The cult, led by the ruthless Rohan, will stop at nothing to expand their empire and destroy anyone who stands in their way. But Aria is not alone in her quest to overthrow the leaders and save Far, a healer who has been targeted by the cult's dark spirits.**

Here, we have the heroine and profession identified, and a clear description of her and her current life. We also use power words such as 'sinister,' 'ruthless,' 'destroy,' and overthrow.' This gives the reader a sense of excitement and peril within the narrative.

The second paragraph is:

> **With the help of Caden, a powerful ally she meets on her journey, Aria learns about the cult's dark history and the key to her own magical abilities. As she grows in strength and courage, she becomes a target for the cult's death threats. But Aria refuses to give up, even when faced with overwhelming odds. With the guidance of the goddess Luna, Aria must find the strength to escape the cult and reclaim her freedom once and for all.**

We are starting to world-build here. We have also added in a problem and some conflict to ramp up the excitement in the reader.

A technique we love to use in blurbs is to **ask questions** at the end of a blurb. The first one is general, and the final one is the real kicker. You want to end on a high, where the reader must buy your book to find out the answers to these questions.

> **Can Aria and Caden overcome the dangers of the cult and outwit Rohan and his followers, or will they succumb to the threats against them?**

Now, use the 'your turn' page in the workbook to write the blurb for your novel.

Plotting - Useful Tools To Help You Further

In this section, we will highlight some tools that make a difference when planning and writing your novel.

Scrivener

The first one we cover in the workbook is a piece of software called Scrivener. This is the go-to app for writers of all kinds and is used every day by best-selling novelists.

What Scrivener offers you is the ability to write your text in any order, in large sections or small. So if you have a great idea but don't know exactly where to put it at that moment in time then you can write it down on Scrivener and decide later. You can build your manuscript piece by piece, idea by idea.

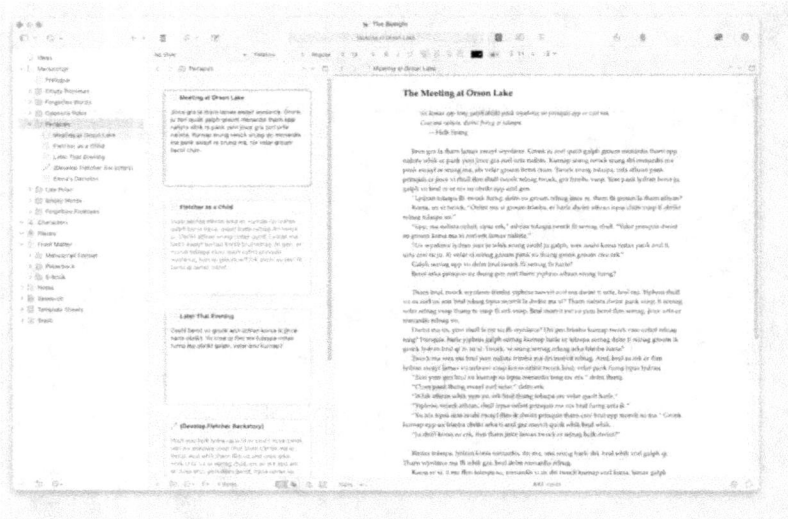

Scrivener lets you write fragments of your story, cultivate every last detail and then lets you restructure later. You can reorder everything you write. If you decide that the contents of a chapter need to be later on in the story then you can reorder the chapters with the drag-and-drop feature.

You can also use Scrivener to conduct your research in the background. You can open it up so it sits right next to your work. This helps you to check for consistency when you are describing a scene from a photograph you have found.

With Scrivener, you can compile everything you have written into a single document for printing and publishing. You can also download in different formats such as PDF, Word or plain text. All in all, Scrivener is a great tool if you are planning as you go along. Or you have those key scenes in your head that you can't seem to order straight away. Scrivener helps to get them out of your head and onto the page – you can order them how you see fit later on.

Plottr

Plottr is another piece of software we recommend you check out. Plottr offers more visual planners to create their manuscripts by using story cards to write on. With these cards, they can arrange and rearrange their scenes, plots and character arcs. It's like having a digital cork board at your disposal.

You can colour-coordinate your storylines so they stay organised. Also, you can flip the timeline horizontally or vertically to make it easier to tag your story cards onto it.

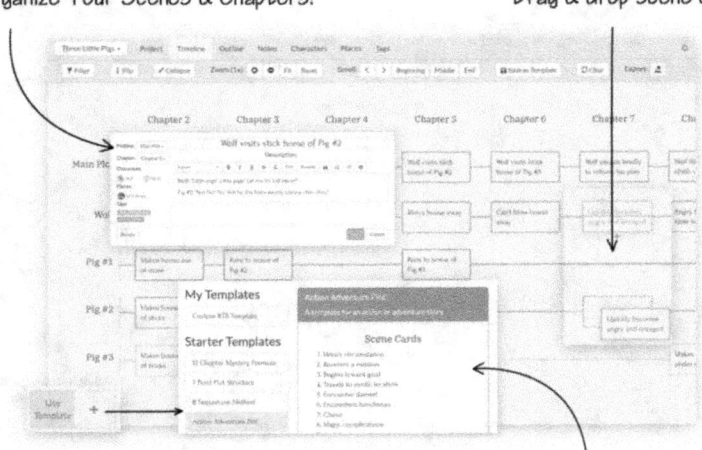

Plottr offers you the ability to see your storyline at a glance. It generates a clean outline of it so you can review, edit or export it as a first draft.

Plottr also comes with lots of templates. These are based on proven storytelling structures (such as the three-act structure we use in our workbook). This helps you to move through your story with the beats and character arcs in all the right places.

Plottr is the better software if you are more visual in your planning, and prefer to use a digital form of notecards.

Both Scrivener and Plottr are well worth investing in, depending on which type of planner you are. Even 'pantsers' will get some value out of using a software programme to compartmentalise their ideas and move towards a first draft.

Bestselling Book Covers

In our opinion, the age-old adage of *'you should never judge a book by its cover'* is wrong.

It is exactly what readers will do. The first impression your readers get of your book is the front cover. It has to make the best first impression it can make. Your front cover has to convey the genre, the style and the main ingredients of your novel all in one 8 by 5-inch space. You must get it right, and to do that there are several things you need to consider.

You should outsource your book covers to a professional designer who specialises in your genre.

The only exception is if you are a graphic designer by trade. Cover design is very technical and an art form in itself. It is not as easy as it may look, positioning images and text, and making sure you integrate them to make the cover immersive. Not to mention the quality of the software you will need to buy. You must also have a comprehensive understanding of how this software works to be able to create a decent front cover/wrap for your book.

You are only going to hurt your sales and your reputation as a serious author if you try to create your own cover. We've seen some very unprofessional-looking front covers in our time. The quality of image composition and choice of typography isn't good enough to compete with the million-sellers in your niche.

This is not to say that you shouldn't get involved in some way with the creation of your book cover. We enjoy this process, giving ideas to our cover designer and receiving drafts back when they show us what they have created. Being creatives, this process is super exciting!

To get the ball rolling with your cover creation, you first select your cover designer.

You then send them images you have found that best sum up your novel's theme. The colour palette of fantasy fiction tends to include purples, silvers, blues and shiny/sparkly effects.

Many fantasy fiction book covers feature elements of magic, such as dragons, unicorns, and other mythical creatures. Fantasy stories often take place in sprawling, fantastical landscapes, and depict the hero as strong, noble and brave, and the villain as evil, menacing and cruel.

You should pick 2-3 different images from bestselling books in your niche, similar in tone to your novel. Then send them off to your cover designer so they can gauge a general understanding of what your vision is.

Ensure you instruct them to **'emulate, not copy'** these images. You can get into serious trouble if you copy someone else's work. Moreover, if they are million-selling authors then you can guarantee someone will notice if you have ripped off their front cover design.

Ask your cover designer to use the same colour palette or font type, line and word spacing. Say to them, "This is the vibe that I want, these are some images that I want to include in my cover, but can you work your magic?" By submitting a clear idea of what you want to be on your cover, your designer will be able to create a professional-looking cover for you.

Your aim when having your book cover designed is to ensure the quality fits in with the genre. You don't want your cover to stand out as being against what the reader expects in this genre. Your book should blend in amongst bestsellers. Then your reader will believe you belong there too, which you do.

In the workbook, we have collated nine different front covers of best-selling books in the fantasy fiction genre:

As you can see they all look very professional, and fit in together as being from the same genre.

None of them look like romance novels, right? You can see the general trend is what we have already identified – purples, silvers, blues and shiny/sparkly elements. The focus of a fantasy fiction novel is to show good versus evil. The vibe of the covers fits this idea. We need to evoke feelings of power and overcoming the darkness. There is no time to waste on jaunty fonts and bright, fluffy and soft colours.

Now, take a closer look at page 143 of the workbook. Here we have the front covers again, but we have slotted in our own professionally designed cover for our example novel, **'Goddess Of The Moon:'**

Can you see how it fits in with these other covers? This is not us blowing our own trumpet. This is us showing you an example of how, with the right direction, your cover designer can create a cover that meets the brief. If you didn't notice it on the previous page then our work here is done.

You might be thinking, "I can't afford to spend hundreds of pounds on a front cover.' We hear you, and this is a very valid point.

The great thing is that you have options of different price points for your cover. **You do not have to spend hundreds on a cover unless you feel you want to.** The cover we had designed for **'Goddess Of The Moon'** cost us $10 only. We used a professional cover designer on a website called Fiverr to design this. It only took 24 hours.

If you wanted to spend a little bit more, you can use a website called 99designs. This is what we use for our historical fiction series, starting with book 1 - **'Shona'**, and then moving through to book 2

– **'Meet Me At 10'**, and then book 3 – **'The Beach House'**. Each cover cost £150.

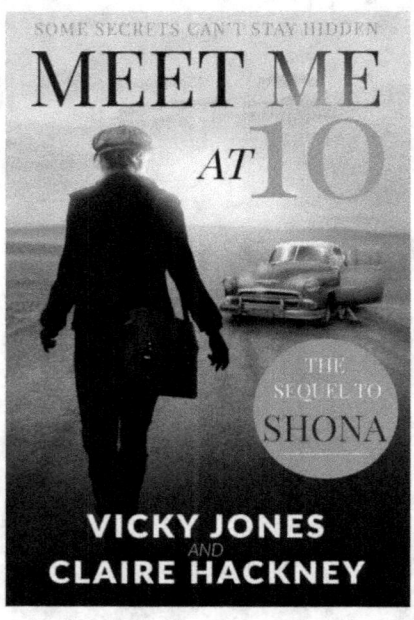

For the DI Rachel Morrison series, starting with **'The Burying Place'**, we used a designer called Stuart Bache from Books Covered. Each cover is £500. For this price, you also get the eBook cover JPEG and the paperback wrap PDF, plus 3 digital images for your marketing.

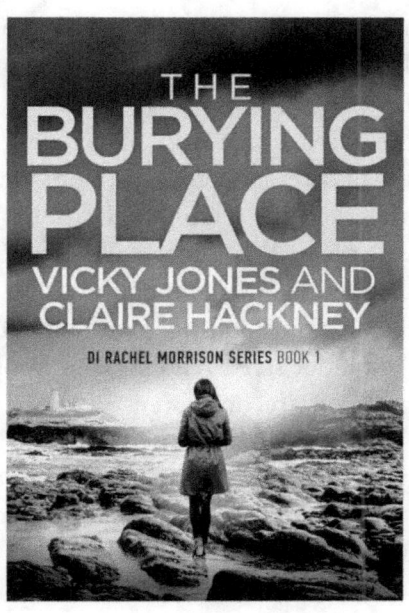

In the images above, you can see the quality of each cover and the points of difference with each one. **The key takeaway is that you can find a designer for every budget,** depending on your requirements.

It is a simple fact though that you get what you pay for. We can say with no hesitation that the best quality, from a user experience point of view and product quality, was Stuart Bache at Books Covered. His service is exceptional. From consultation on the design to revisions, right through to the final order, we experienced nothing short of fantastic care and attention to detail. Yes, it was at the top of our budget, but the results speak for themselves.

We also know that a vast amount of the top-selling authors use Books Covered. If you go on any writer's Facebook group, including the SPF (Self-Publishing Formula) group, his name is always at the top of recommendations.

Our last word on this subject is this – if you invest in your cover, to the best of your financial ability, your readers will assume that the quality inside the book is also top-notch.

If you scrimp on the cover design price, or worse, create your own cover, your readers will take one look at a poorly designed cover and think you also scrimped on the editing and proofreading. They will assume you think so little of the reader's experience that you are selling them shoddy goods. You might counter that with an argument that the quality of your plotting, planning and writing is still sound, and once the reader starts reading your book they will see how fantastic a writer you are, and forget all about your cover.

But, our answer to that is simple. **If your reader doesn't ever pick your book up because the cover is poor, how will they ever discover this?**

Self-Publishing Vs Traditional Publishing

Self-publishing was once known as 'vanity publishing.'

That meant you would complete your manuscript and then send it off to a printing firm to get copies made. Worse still, you would send your manuscript off to a company that would charge you the earth to "publish" your novel for you.

Yes, you were published, but the company you paid £4000+ to, didn't have the marketing links to get your book sold widely, and most definitely not globally.

Then the internet evolved and everything changed.

Self-publishing

If you don't want to go through a traditional publishing house, you can use online publishing platforms.

You would do this if you want to keep full control over your copyrights and more royalty percentage. These are companies such as

Draft to Digital, Ingram Spark, and of course Amazon KDP. With these companies, you can publish your book globally.

Self-publishing is where an author takes full responsibility for the writing, editing, proofreading and marketing of their book. They do all this without the financial backing of a publishing house.

You, as the author, will hire your own editor, proofreader and marketing team and give them your requirements. This will come at a price for you to pay upfront.

You must ensure you hire a professional editor. This can either be for:

A **copy edit** - they do a basic run through your manuscript and offer you advice on improvements

or

A **developmental edit** - which is much more in-depth and offers you much more in the way of a structural edit.

A developmental editor will cost you more, but they are doing more work so it stands to reason. Research this person and their company well. There are an awful lot of people who say they are an editor, but only give you a cheap version of a "second pair of eyes" ran over your manuscript.

You need an editor who is not shy of letting you have the hard truth about your novel. They will also be supportive enough to give you all the pointers you need.

They will look out for:

- Inconsistencies
- Plot holes
- Loose characterisations

- "Going nowhere" plots that will turn your reader off.

They intend to make your novel the best version of itself. You may need to send your manuscript off to them a few times. This will ensure you get your novel into its best possible shape.

Next, comes the **proofreader**. A proofreader should be the last step before your manuscript goes to beta readers, or to print – whichever you decide.

A good proofreader will check again:

- Inconsistencies on a grammatical level
- If you are writing in US English or British English
- You remain consistent so 'colour' doesn't become 'color' at any point)

They will also do a complete spelling, punctuation and grammar check using their own eyes, and the best software money can buy to assist them.

When it comes to editing and proofreading, you may be asking *"how do I find a good one?"* You can either go off recommendations on social media. You must ensure though that the person recommending them has actually used them. Don't accept they are just buddies with them. You can search on reputable sites that offer these services.

Or you could use someone in your circle who is professionally qualified. However, even the best English teachers in the world are not proofreaders or editors.

Being an editor or proofreader entails gaining professional qualifications in this niche. It is a specialised field, so pay it the respect it deserves and hire a professional.

Most editors and proofreaders charge by the word. You must

consider this factor before you submit your novel. If you know that there is a lot of fluff in your novel, trim that down first before you submit. **You may be paying a few hundred pounds more for those extra unnecessary words if you don't.**

Now you've had your novel edited and proofread, you are ready to release it to the world. You can now upload it in paperback or eBook format onto whichever platform suits your requirements.

Amazon - Kindle Direct Publishing (KDP)
If Amazon is your thing then you can upload it to their platform, KDP (Kindle Direct Publishing). You can upload an eBook, a paperback and a hardback version of your book on KDP.

Submissions are free, as are revisions to the manuscript or cover. You cannot, however, change the title, subtitle, trim size or paper colour **after submission**. You can also if you want to, enrol your eBook into their Kindle Select programme. By allowing Amazon to have your eBook exclusive to them they pay you a royalty for every digital page read of your book.

This has its positives: it is an extra income for you. The negatives are you cannot put your eBook anywhere else for sale, i.e. on Ingram Spark or Draft to Digital.

Ingram Spark

With Ingram Spark, there is a charge for uploading an eBook and paperback. At the time of writing this guidebook, eBooks were $29 to upload and paperbacks/hardbacks were $49. You have to pay this fee again for every revision hereafter. If you are uploading an eBook and a paperback/hardback at the same time it will cost $49. It makes financial sense to upload an eBook and paperback if you have both ready at the same time.

Draft to Digital

For Draft to Digital, there is no charge for submitting either an eBook or paperback. You can only revise the interiors every 90 days though. Any changes within 90 days will incur a charge in the form of tokens you can buy.

There are other online book-selling platforms. The three outlined above are the three we use, so it made sense to highlight them to you. Using all three ensures we have three separate streams of revenue. This makes financial sense, as if you put all your eggs in one basket you may struggle if one stops selling your book for whatever reason.

Traditional publishing

Traditional book publishing is when an author signs a contract with a publishing house. In return, they agree to print, publish, market and sell the book for you through bookstores.

The publishing house purchases the rights to your book, through the contract they agree with you. You then receive a royalty payment for any and every sale of your book made.

This is the old-school way of seeing your book in print. It is, however, very difficult to get a publishing deal. The publishing houses are very selective of what books they want to spend their money on. To get a deal, you must send your manuscript to them, or the first three chapters and a synopsis. It all depends on what the requirements are from that particular publishing house. The upshot is though if they like the sound of your novel they will offer you a deal. If you are only three chapters in and they like how it sounds, they may offer you an advance payment for you to finish it.

Traditional book publishing is the ultimate endorsement of your writing ability. A huge, powerful publisher likes your stuff – how amazing is that? But don't get too hung up if you can't get one to read your book. Self-publishing gives you the ability to see your work in print.

The main difference between self and traditional publishing is the amount of royalty you receive. Self-publishers will keep 50-70% (depending on which online publishing format you use) of the royalty from each book sold. Traditionally published authors will typically receive 15-20% royalty for each book sold.

This is because self-publishers have paid to do all the work on their manuscript. They keep all the rights to their book. Traditionally published authors relinquish all their rights to the book. They take a smaller royalty to "pay" the publishing house back for the costs they will have incurred to bring the book to market.

This all depends on the particular deal you sign though. If a publishing house approaches you, you must hire an expert lawyer to look over the contract before you sign anything. If you relinquish all the rights to the book without expert advice then you are putting yourself in a very vulnerable position.

One day your book might become a film. You must show due diligence before going into any contract signing. Regardless of how many noughts they offer you.

Self-publishing Vs Traditional publishing - the pros and cons of each

The pros of self-publishing are:

PROS

- Full control over your manuscript.
- Higher royalty rates.
- Unlimited amount of books you can publish.
- You are your own boss.

The cons of self-publishing are:

CONS

- Potentially high upfront costs.
- Risk of selling less books.
- Less understanding by others of what you do for a living.
- Lots of process to learn and master.

The pros of traditional publishing are:

PROS

- No upfront costs.
- Potentially sell more books.
- Social credibility.
- Editing, proofreading and marketing all done for you.

The cons of traditional publishing are:

CONS

- **Extremely competitive.**
- **Lengthy process.**
- **Limited creative control over your book.**
- **Lower royalty payments.**

Limited creative control over your book includes the cover design. This means, if you receive a cover design draft and hate it, you will have little say in it. Unless you get that part drawn up into the contract and have the agreement from them that you can offer your input into this cover design.

Authors get so excited and feel grateful they have a book deal that they will allow the publishing house to use their professional expertise to make these judgements on cover design. You have to decide how important these issues are to you and go from there with your contract negotiations.

Whichever method of publishing you go for, both have their positives and negatives. Choose the one that's right for you and go from there.

Bonuses

Since the start of our writing journey, we have always believed that having professional, talented and expert editors and proofreaders on our team is the key to success. We know this through bitter experiences.

The first time we sent a manuscript to a proofreader we were completely scammed by someone we thought was a professional.

They returned our manuscript with only the first eight pages proofread (a cursory glance over the pages, we surmised) and the final eight. They hadn't glanced at any between. We know this because our proofreader made no notes or amendments to these pages. No sections with the choice to accept or reject their suggestion for a change in the sentence structure or word spelling. They had also made it so we were unable to contact them and we had to pay to get it redone elsewhere.

We have to add in here that we do blame ourselves a little for not checking they had completed the job. But when you hire who you think is a professional then you have some faith, right? You can never do enough checks though, as we've said in the previous section on editors and proofreaders. Rookie mistake, we admit, and we know now we were easy meat for the unscrupulous proofreader who took every penny of the £800 fee we paid.

A hard lesson to learn, but one of the most valuable as now we check everything. We vowed that day never to let that happen to us again. From then, we tried a few different editors and proofreaders out with samples first before we committed.

One of the best things to come out of all this was the next proofreader we found was, and is, brilliant. We have used **Melanie at Inspire Envisioning** for each fiction book we have written. She has been magnificent and is a joy to work with. Also, **Gary at Bubblecow**, who is our editor, has been fantastic to work with. He offers complete and concise advice on each manuscript we send him. He develops the story with us so that it hits all the right notes for the reader.

To this day, we have never had a single review, in many hundreds of reviews across our entire back catalogue of fiction books, that has mentioned typos, editing mistakes or inaccuracies. **Proof indeed that our team does their job well.**

Having a strong team around us helps us get excited about each fiction book we write and publish.

Because we are so confident in our team, we want to offer you an exclusive discount on their services.

There is nothing whatsoever in it for us, we do not make a cut from it, or are in any affiliate deal with them at all. We want to offer you this discount for the simple reason that we do not want you getting ripped off by substandard editors and proofreaders like we were.

If you have your own trusty band of brothers already set up then go with them. But if you are starting from scratch then we cannot recommend Gary and Melanie highly enough. Our reputation is on the line here, so we would never sell you short.

To receive your 10% discount on editing services, all you have to do is email Gary at Bubblecow.com. Put the code HACKNEYANDJONES10 in the subject box, or quote it in the body of your email.

> **2**   <u>**GET IT EDITED:**</u>
>
> Use the discount code 'HACKNEYANDJONES10' in the subject line and in your email to receive a 10% discount on your editing if you use our approved editor.
>
> Contact Gary at Bubblecow.com here: Bubblecow.com or scan the QR code below.
>
>    Affordable book editing services.
>
>   Providing professional editing services for serious writers since 2007.

To receive your 10% discount on proofreading services, email Melanie at inspireenvisioning.com. Put the code HACKNEYANDJONES10 in the subject box or quote it in the body of your email.

3   GET IT PROOFREAD:

Use the discount code 'HACKNEYANDJONES10' in the subject line and in your email to receive a 10% discount on your editing if you use our approved proofreader.

Contact Melanie at Inspire Envisioning here:

Inspireenvisioning.com/tag/proofreading

or scan the QR code on the left.

We'd also like to help you to promote your novel once it's published. This is another bonus as a thank you from us .
As soon as your novel is live on Amazon, contact us at

vicky.hackneyandjones@gmail.com
Or go to
hackneyandjones.com

We promise to share the link to your novel with our Twitter, Instagram and email list.

This is an audience of over 140,000 followers. We'd be more than proud to show off a book that's been through our planning system and get you as many sales as possible.

To help you become more confident with the whole self-publishing process, don't forget to check out Publisher Rocket.

On this website, there are lots of tutorials that will explain the process to you in a lot more detail. Publisher Rocket helps you to choose the best categories for your book to feature in. This will give it the best possible chance of finding its way up the charts to bestseller status in its category. We use Publisher Rocket all the time and it has become a key piece of our publishing kit.

Course Offer

This section at the end is a little extra from us to you.

If you want some more in-depth support, more of a one-to-one approach to help you get from a blank page to a full novel outline then **we can help you with that.**

Our online course is the ideal solution for authors to speed up the entire process of writing.

Sometimes we need somebody friendly to explain things on a more one-to-one basis. Our online course does that. We go more in-depth to bring out your brilliance in our unique course.

Our mission statement is to motivate you to write your novel outline in 21 days or less.

We know how hard this process can be to do alone, but with our online course, we are right by your side every step of the way. We even help you to experiment across different genres to maximise your earning potential. So, if you are a romance writer who wants to move into horror, or science fiction writing with a bit of historical thrown in, we can help you understand the different requirements of each genre.

If you've liked what we've done so far (and we're hoping that you have if you've come this far), you will love what's involved in our online course.

For a one-off investment, you get all the following:

COURSE OFFER

FEATURE	COURSE	WORKBOOK
GENRE BUNDLE - **FANTASY**	✓	✓
THE COMPLETE **PLAN**	✓	✓
10% **EDITOR DISCOUNT**	✓	✓
10% **PROOFREADER DISCOUNT**	✓	✓
SYNOPSIS **TEMPLATE**	✓	✓
BLURB **TEMPLATE**	✓	✓
BOOK COVER DESIGN **ADVICE**	✓	✓
WHAT TO DO NOW	✓	✓
STEP-BY-STEP **TUTORIALS**	✓	✓
MARKETING **YOUR BOOK**	✓	✓
AMAZON ADS **COURSE**	✓	✓
CHARACTERS - IN-DEPTH/BACKSTORY/TRAITS AND QUIRKS	✓	✗

COURSE OFFER

FEATURE	COURSE	WORKBOOK
LOCATIONS - WHERE/ HOW TO RESEARCH THESE	✓	✗
RESEARCH - MAKE YOUR NOVEL COME ALIVE	✓	✗
PLOT TWISTS - IN-DEPTH	✓	✗
CHARACTER ARCS - BECOME THE EXPERT	✓	✗
THE WALLOP SCENE SECRETS - BEGIN YOUR NOVEL WITH A BANG!	✓	✗
ENDINGS - THE COMPLETE GUIDE TO A JAW-DROPPER!	✓	✗
15-MINUTE STRATEGY CALL WITH ONE OF US BEFORE YOU START SO WE CAN PLAN TOGETHER	✓	✗
24-HOUR ACCESS TO OUR PRIVATE FACEBOOK GROUP FOR COURSE DELEGATES	✓	✗
IMPACT SCENES	✓	✗
WRITING DIALOGUE	✓	✗

COURSE OFFER

FEATURE	COURSE	WORKBOOK
SHOW NOT TELL	✓	✗
1-MONTH PROMOTION ON OUR SOCIAL MEDIA PLATFORMS AND PROMOTION ON OUR EMAIL LIST	✓	✗
ALL THE BACK-END KEYWORDS YOU WILL NEED WHEN YOU UPLOAD YOUR BOOK ON AMAZON - TO ENSURE YOUR BOOK GETS FOUND	✓	✗
DOWNLOADS OF ALL OF OUR FICTION BOOKS	✓	✗
CATEGORY RESEARCH DONE FOR YOU - WE GIVE YOU THE SECRET CATEGORIES FOR YOUR NICHE TO HELP YOU GET THAT BESTSELLER STATUS!	✓	✗
WE BUY YOUR BOOK!	✓	✗
MORE WAYS TO MAKE MONEY WITH YOUR BOOKS	✓	✗
HOW TO UPLOAD YOUR BOOK TO AMAZON KDP	✓	✗
MAKE YOUR BOOK MORE VISIBLE TO YOUR READERS	✓	✗

COURSE OFFER

FEATURE	COURSE	WORKBOOK
ALL FICTION GENRES COVERED - INCLUDING: • CRIME • ROMANCE • SCI-FI • HISTORICAL • YOUNG ADULT • MILITARY • WOMEN'S FICTION • FANTASY • PARANORMAL • HORROR • COSY MYSTERY • PSYCHOLOGICAL/SUSPENSE/THRILLER • ACTION AND ADVENTURE • EROTICA	✓	✗
30-DAY NO QUIBBLE MONEY BACK GUARANTEE - ABSOLUTE PEACE OF MIND!	✓	✗
£50 BACK IF YOU DON'T MAKE 10 SALES IN 2 WEEKS - WE'RE *THAT* CONFIDENT IN THIS COURSE'S SUCCESS FOR YOU!	✓	✗
FULL REFUND ON THE COST OF YOUR WORKBOOK IF YOU GO ON TO PURCHASE OUR ONLINE WRITING COURSE!	✓	✗
RECEIVE 20% OF THE COURSE PRICE BACK AS A REFUND WHEN YOU SUBMIT A COMPLETE SYNOPSIS OF YOUR NOVEL AT THE END OF THE COURSE	✓	✗

As you can see from the comparisons, you get so much more for your money with the online course. One of the key features is that we will refund you the cost of your fantasy fiction workbook when you buy the online course.

So, **there is nothing to lose for you** – your workbook is your opportunity to try us out first.

We also promise to buy your published novel – **we guarantee you your first sale!**

Our online course goes the extra mile for you.

We will give you all the backend keywords for your book to use when you upload it, and help you with category research. There is so much added value in the online course, as you will see in the images.

We will also show you more ways of making money with your book. You will automatically get access to all the other genres that we're doing in the form of downloadable PDFs of the workbooks we create in these niches.

If our online course sounds good to you then go to www.hackneyandjones.com to register your interest.

Contact Us

Thank you for reading this guide to your fantasy fiction workbook. We sincerely hope it has added value and helped you to understand how the workbook works and given you extra food for thought as you fill it in.

As you go through the process of writing your book, and marketing it when it is published, keep tagging us on social media with your book cover, blurbs, or anything at all to do with your book and we'll share your posts on our platforms.

You can find us on all the socials below:

Join the Journey on Social Media!
Follow and say Hello!

 vickyjones7
clairehac

 HackneyandJones

 vickytjones
clairehackneyauthor

 VickyJonesWriter
ClaireHackneyAuthor

We want you to succeed and completely believe in you. The whole point of us creating these writing workbooks is because we feel so passionate that people who think the reason they can't write books is that they can't see a way forward.

We believe that this is simply not true.

Where there is a formula for success, there is a pathway through anything.

This Workbook Goes With The Guidebook You Are Reading

The ultimate novel writing planner with a secret formula to hook your readers in from the very first page. Effortlessly create a magical story from scratch using creative writing templates that will catapult you from blank page to publishing a fantasy novel that sells.

www.ingramcontent.com/pod-product-compliance
Lightning Source LLC
Chambersburg PA
CBHW050028130526
44590CB00042B/2184